RIDING THE FENCE LINES

Riding the Fences That Define the Margins of Religious Tolerance

Bernie Keating

with

Rabbi Gordon, Dr. S. Amjad Hussain, Father Michael Kelly
Rev. Joel P. Miller and Dr. Seigen Yamaoka

ISBN: 0-9710723-4-5

Library of Congress Control Number: 2003114674

Copyright 2003 Bernie Keating

Published by BWD Publishing LLC - Toledo, OH

Printed and bound in the United States of America

ABOUT THE AUTHORS

Bernie Keating was raised in cattle towns in South Dakota in the shadow of the Sioux Indian Reservation. He served as a naval officer aboard destroyers during the Korean War, and then had a long career as an executive in a multi-national company, where his world-wide travels brought him in contact with many of the great religions of the world.

S. Amjad Hussain, is past president of the Islamic Center of Greater Toledo, one of the largest and progressive Islamic Centers in America. He is a clinical professor of Thoracic and Cardiovascular surgery and an op-ed columnist for the daily Blade of Toledo, Ohio. A renowned explorer and award winning photographer, he has explored and photographed the length of the Indus River in Tibet and Pakistan

He has written extensively on Islam and Central Asian politics for American audiences. He is the author of eight books including Of Home and Country (1996), The Taliban and Beyond (2001) and the Ornate Goblet (2003).

Rabbi Paul Gordon, an immigrant from Canada, came to be a rabbi in a circuitous path from Reform to Orthodox to Conservative Jew during his formulative and college years, and now calls himself a "Reform-Conserv-Oxdy" Jew as leader of the Beth Shalom Synagogue in Modesto, California.

Father Michael Kelly was raised in Tipperary County, Ireland, entered the seminary to become ordained as a Catholic Priest, and then was sent as a missionary to several parishes in northern California. An avid sportsman, he founded, and is called the Father of Youth Soccer in the San Joaquin Valley, and is also a karate Black Belt.

Dr. Seigen Yamaoka found his religious faith as a youth in a Japanese Interment Camp during World War Two, and has a Litt. D. from Ryukoku University in Jodo Shinshu Studies. He is leader of the Buddhist Temple of Oakland, one of the larger Buddhist congregations in California, and he reminds us of an ancient rule, "Hate is not overcome by hatred, hatred is overcome by love."

Reverend Joel P. Miller is rector of St. Francis of Assisi Episcopal Church in Turlock, California. As a Christian educator, he served for nearly two decades as a missionary in the predominantly Muslim North African countries of Morocco, and Tunisia, where he learned to conciliate as a bridge between differing faiths.

PREFACE

Is there a God? I don't know and neither do you. I have listened to a lifetime of sermons and seldom was this question tackled head-on; they mostly just recite how much He loves us. The exception was a young priest who gave a sermon questioning the existence of God, and then a week later he attempted suicide, recovered, left the priesthood, married, and is now a lawyer in Texas. So the question is not one to trifle with.

This discourse will be about God, more or less. How am I qualified since I have no religious credentials? Neither did Plato who worshipped his Greek Gods. Nor did Abraham or his father, Terah, Semites who left Babylon, crossed the River Euphrates, and established themselves as the Hebrews. Gautama (Buddha) had no religious training when he abandoned his wife and fled to a hermit cave for meditation, but the religion he established persists throughout much of the world today. We know virtually nothing about Jesus from the time of his infancy until he started preaching 30 years later. Then came Muhammad who had his first religious encounter in mid-life with the angel Gabriel in a cave of the Arabic desert and founded the Islamic religion. Perhaps each of us has as much expertise as any other, because no one has ever seen God nor has provable evidence of his existence.

If there is a God he certainly passed along conflicting signals. In the four millenniums of recorded history most the great wars were launched by one religious group against another. Have the centuries given us more wisdom? I am Irish-American, so I've been perplexed over the long war in Ireland fought between Catholics and Protestants with both sides bombing women and children while claiming adherence to the teaching of Christ. Nor can I give a solution to Jewish-Palestine war fought for the "Holy Land". What happened in the Balkans where Christians on one side and Muslims on the other brutally murdered the women and children of each other? Nor do we Americans have clean hands with our centuries of genocide against the native Indians. Our Christian ancestors kidnapped blacks in Africa, pressed them into slavery, and then attended Sunday church services. Today we see bombings and shooting on such religious debates as abortion and euthanasia, all in the name of some God. And so it goes.

Don't get defensive; work with me.

Perhaps my credentials, if I have any, are because I have been a first-hand witness to many of the world's religions. I was raised in frontier towns with cowboy "infidels". My mother was a Methodist who learned the King James Bible; my father a Catholic raised with the Baltimore catechism, and I received a dose of both. My playmates in Buffalo Gap were Sioux Indian children whose grandparents spent their youth in nomad tribes on the Dakota prairies, worshipping the lightening and thunder that came from the Black Hills. Over campfires I listened to these old warriors recount their God-like visions of the White Buffalo.

Then as an adult traveling through six continents of the world, I lived and worked with those of the Jewish, Muslim, Orthodox, and Buddhist faith. The more I learned, the more confused I became about the various Gods, and why did He or It make things so complex. Like everyone, I brought the prejudices from my cultural background into a look at religion. So does everyone else including Popes, Rabbi's, Ayatollah, and agnostics; none of us live religion in the abstract; we all come to our own faith in the muddled process of life, each carrying the baggage from our past. Then we dig post holes and string a fence around our territory.

I know about fences. Seems I've been riding fence lines all my life. I was raised in cattle country - worked as a cowboy on the 7-11 ranch west of Buffalo Gap. I'd saddle up with fencing tools and head up the mountains along the western fence line. Good fences made for good neighbors; they kept our stock in and their stock out, but there was always some fence mending to do. With a strong mustang I could reach Wolf Canyon by noon for a biscuit alongside the spring, and then head back along the Calico Canyon fence line. It was a hard and lonely life, and I opted for something else. Then an urban cowboy riding jets around the world, I seemed to be still on the fence lines. As an executive in a multi-national corporation, the tasks and names changed, but I was still in the saddle, riding patrol, and on the hunt.

As we ride through the pastures of our own life, occasionally glancing over the fence at the vistas beyond, we all face our personal search for a God: is there one; if so, what is It's nature and how close a facsimile to a Yahweh, Allah, or Jehovah; is this short life on earth all there is, or is there more? I've been riding those fence lines all my life.

But I don't ride fences by myself. I am joined by five religious leaders. This unique cast includes these co-authors: Dr. S. Amjad Hussain, a Muslim growing up in Pakistan on the Afghan border; Dr. Siegen Yamaoka, who found his Buddhist faith in a World War Two Japanese internment camp; Father Michael Kelly, raised in turbulent war-torn Ireland; Rabbi Paul Gordon, an immigrant from Canada, who became a rabbi in a circuitous path from Reform to Orthodox to Conservative Jew; and The Rev. Joel P. Miller, who lived for two decades as a missionary in Muslim countries of North Africa.

Each tells how they came to their religious faith. Don't under-estimate the challenge these five men faced in telling their stories. They have spent a lifetime in serving others, assisting others through the journey of life; and now they were asked to pause, go beyond the confines of a traditional sermon, reach into their gut, and then share with us a very personal look at their own life.

While their stories differ in reflecting the vast differences in the culture from which they came, a common theme does emerge. Their particular religious faith is a central part of their life, yet the more they understand about other cultures, the more tolerance they develop, and the more they understand their own faith. Dr. Hussain states it this way:

"We all ride fence lines stocked with our own provisions and equipped with our unique tools. In the end our destination, I firmly believe, is the same. We all reach home even if through different routes and taking different paths."

My role is somewhat minor, and as you will see I am provocative and sometimes irreligious. I provide the glue that binds their stories together, and a buffer that permits them all to appear in the same book. Each of these men has spent a lifetime riding the fence lines that define the margins of ethnic and religious tolerance. If you would like to join us in riding those fence lines, saddle up and let's go.

Bernie Keating

CHAPTERS

1

THE OLD SIOUX WARRIOR

No-Water, Billy Thompson, and I rode our ponies down the ravine to Beaver Creek, waded across it with the water knee deep to the horses, and entered the No-Water encampment at the edge of the cottonwood grove on the Sewright ranch. The Sioux grandfather, reclining against a log in the shade alongside the teepee, watched as we dismounted and turned our horses loose. The old man, wearing a solitary eagle in his hair which hung long and straight, smiled and said something in Sioux to his grandson.

"What did he say, George?" I asked.

"He said in the old days when they lived here with Sitting Bull, he had a pinto mare exactly like yours. He's always talking about the old days and the crazy things they worshipped. It's boring. Come on; let's go over to the hay barns and play."

No-Water and Billy were my playmates for the summer. I lived in Buffalo Gap, a town named for the valley that created a passage for the buffalo from the prairie into the Black Hills. The Sioux Indian Reservation was a few miles east on the Dakota prairie. My family lived across from the Sewright ranch, and I spent most hours of the summer over there with his grandson. As a struggling rancher barely keeping his head above water during the rough depression years of the 1930's, Sewright hustled any way

11

he could. One of his enterprises was to butcher sheep and cows during the winter time and take them to the Indian Reservation to sell. He didn't actually sell anything, because the destitute Sioux had nothing. It was a bartering process. He'd give them meat and potatoes, and in return they'd agree to work the following summer on his ranch, where he'd supply them with food and a place to stay. The Stands-Alone family of four spent the summer living in an abandoned rail box car that had been moved to the vacant lot across from our house. Their two children were playmates of my younger sister and brother. Several Sioux males: Percy Kills-a-Warrior, Comes-Again, and John Sitting Bull, would come without their families and live in a shack that was once a hay barn. The No-Water family pitched a teepee alongside the creek that meandered through the ranch. George No-Water's father drove a team of work horses to pull mowing machines during the haying season. The grandfather, I never knew if he had a first name we just called him No-Water, was an old man in his eighties, long past the age of working on the ranch. He sat all day in the shade under the cottonwood trees alongside the teepee. While he understood English when he wanted to, he seldom spoke anything but Sioux, and gradually I learned some of it. When we boys struck his fancy, he would tell us stories about the old days. Often I'd linger with him alongside the campfire, someone to listen to an old man with many memories about life on the plains that no one else wanted to hear.

No-Water had been raised a member of Sitting Bull's tribe that had roamed this country as nomads, living in teepees, and following the buffalo herds. This gap in the mountains was their camping place while the buffalo herds were leaving the Black Hills with the first snows and moving onto the plains where the snows were lighter. The Sioux pitched their teepees alongside the creek in these cottonwood groves and feasted on the plentiful buffalo. Then later in the winter, the tribe would move with the meandering herd out onto the plains and hunker down in protected ravines, sheltered from the blizzards that blew around the north end of the Black Hills.

No-Water was a survivor. He had been with Sitting Bull at the Little

Big Horn when Custer attacked their village. That was sixty years earlier when he was twenty years of age. It was a confused battle with women, children, warriors, soldiers everywhere. After the battle he fled with Sitting Bull into Canada. A dozen years later when he was returning with his squaw and child to the reservation during the cold winter, he was with the Sioux at Wounded Knee. His wife and son were slaughtered by the US cavalry as he watched helplessly from a ridge a mile away. He married again, and his grandson was my playmate.

In those days, we whites used the term "Squaw" to identify an Indian wife. It was a derogatory reference. There is currently a semantic debate over what term should be used, but until that is settled I shall use the English word "wife" out of respect for the many fine Indian women I have known.

His stories of the battles came from the old warrior over the campfire as he turned hunks of meat on the crude spit. This night he felt like talking, and it came forth in a combination of Sioux and his blend of English. I understood most of it, and George translated the rest.

"Did he ever go up into the Black Hills when he was a boy?" I asked. The answer was a resounding no. The Black Hills were a hostile place where few Indians ventured except in an armed hunting party; it was full of bears and other prey that attacked them and spooked their horses. Then there was the thunder and lightening. The old warrior's eyes closed as he mumbled something about these Spirits. He had once climbed the mountain we call Bear Butte, there he was close to those Spirits, and he saw visions of the White Buffalo. A cloud came and the thunder roared and the lightening struck the trees, then he fled down the mountain in a rain storm, never to return. He was telling me of the Vision and these Spirits as he turned the spit over the fire. Then George's father returned from his day on the ranch and told me I must go home before my parents worried, because a storm was on the way.

The storm hit. Lightening bolts off the high peaks turned night into day, thunderclaps shook the foundations of our house, then the rain and wind uprooted trees that crashed to the ground outside my bedroom window. These were No-Water's angry Spirits, and I could believe in them just as I did in the white man's church-God I heard about on Sundays. Was No-Water's vision of a White Buffalo, his symbol of hope, a God? I had my own dreams, too. Perhaps we each search for our White Buffalo.

But I am ahead of myself in relating this story of the Sioux and their Spirits. Four thousand years earlier than this, half way around the world in Mesopotamia which is now Iraq, a tribe of wandering Semite nomads were led by their tribal Patriarch, Terah, into a new land. There his son, Abraham, found his God, Jehovah, in a vision on a mountain top. He established a race and religion known today as the Hebrews and the Jewish religion. Like the nomad Sioux tribe that were uprooted from their homeland time and again, the Jewish people lived as wandering nomads for seventeen hundred years. Let's join them in Chapter Two.

2

JUDAISM

"The monotheistic religion of the Jews that traces its roots to Mesopotamia in 2000 BC, having its ethical, ceremonial, and legal foundations in the precepts of the Old Testament and in the teachings and commentaries of the rabbis as found chiefly in the Talmud; their God is Jehovah."

Perhaps no people know more about "fence lines" than the Jewish, who have spent four thousand years trying to establish their own safe haven, a territory they could call their own, and spent most of those four millenniums as nomads wandering around the world. The story of the Jewish people and religion is central to understanding several of the major religions of the world. Both Christianity and Islam can trace many of their religious traditions to Judaism.

The Jewish people have their roots in Mesopotamia, now part of Iraq, where it started with a Semitic tribe of that era. Sometime about 2000 *BCE (historians now place it between 1800-1900BCE), a man named Terah took his son Abraham and family and emigrated from the city of Ur in Babylon. (Four millenniums later this city of Ur in Iraq would be a battle site in the Gulf War of 1991.) Crossing the River Euphrates, they traveled six hundred miles north to the southern part of what is now Turkey. They became identified as "Hebrews", the people "who crossed over". The Hebrew word for this is Iv'rim.

*Some writers use BCE "Before Common Era", and CE for "Common Era" instead of BC and AD to avoid using a religious connotation

It was this patriarch Abraham who had an encounter with God, "Jehovah", who proposes a covenant with Abraham. If he will follow the commandments of God, the descendants of Abraham will become his chosen people. Thus the foundation of the Jewish religion was set, and "the three founding fathers of Judaism are Abraham, his son Isaac, and Isaac's son Jacob." This religion has survived through thousands of years. During that time they survived intact, having lived through the following cycles of several civilizations

Pagan World: The earliest beginnings were during an era when Pagan religions flourished throughout the world. The Hebrews began as wandering nomads among such nations as Babylonia, Assyria, Phoenicia, Egypt, and Persia during a seventeen-hundred year span of time, finally settling in Jerusalem. With the compression of time, it is difficult for us to grasp how long that is: it is equal to the time from the Roman Empire to the present day. Through that long journey, finally emerging as the Twelve Tribes of Canaan, this confederation of nomad tribes were kicked from pillar to post through countries of Asia Minor and Northern Africa. They gradually defined the fence lines of the Jewish people and the Judaic religion.

Greco-Roman Period: This cycle began with Alexandra the Great of Macedonia, who was on the march in quest of a new empire. Some time after Moses lead the Israelites out of Egypt, the Greeks invaded the Aegean Peninsula, and the Jewish people came under their heel. After the Greeks, the Roman legions ruled the Jews, but after the Roman Empire collapsed, the Jews still remained.

The Scattering: This cycle (properly called the "Diaspora", the Greek word for scattering) began when the Jews were driven from Jerusalem by the Babylonians in the sixth century. The Jewish people were fragmented throughout the world without a homeland until the founding of the State of Israel in 1948.

Middle Ages: This was a twelve hundred year ordeal for the Jew, who survived in the ghetto in Europe, then emerged with the renaissance to become a central player in much of the evolving western civilization. During this era there were other Jews living in Spain, North Africa, and elsewhere.

Most of the other great nations of four thousand years ago have disappeared, but the Jewish people have survived intact. How did the Jewish religious faith survive through the thousands of years and various civilizations that came, and then crumbled. Perhaps for two reasons, one is their faith that they are, indeed, a chosen people; the second is the creation of a religious code, the Talmud, which served as a unifying force. This Talmud in its present form has ruled the Jewish religion for close to fifteen hundred years.

After their beginnings with Abraham, about 2000 BCE, the Hebrews became a tribe of wandering nomads. Later they were enslaved in Egypt. Around 1200 BCE, Moses led them out of bondage and into the Sinai desert. They wandered around the Sinai for forty years. It is here that Moses gives his people the Ten Commandments and other Mosaic code, which are the pillars upon which Judaism rests. During this time in the desert, this new law, the Torah, is revealed to the Jews. "The first five books of the Hebrew Bible comprise the Torah and are regarded as Judaism's central document." Eventually it evolved into the Talmud, which embraces the entire range of Jewish law, and in addition contains materials on medicine, astronomy, meteorology, agriculture, and many other subjects affecting human life.

During the first millennium CE, there was a long period of gestation; during that time, Jewish thought was crystallized into their body of knowledge, the Talmud, or "learning". Then the Talmud began a series of evolutionary changes: first by a Moroccan named Alfasi; another by a North African, Maimonides; and finally in 1565 CE a third revision by Joseph Cargo, in Jerusalem. It was this changing and growing Talmud that provided the guidelines by which the homeland-less Jewish race and faith survived through the centuries of Ghetto's and a scattering throughout the world.

Finally the Jew came into the modern world and America; here the institutions of rabbi, prayer, and synagogue are again changing. The rabbi is no longer the interpreter of Talmudic Judaism, but a counselor and interfaith mediator; prayer is no longer exclusively personal intercession with God, but praise of the Creator; the synagogue is no longer exclusively a place of worship, but also a social community for expressing one's ties to Judaism. Portions of the Talmud dealing with dietary and ritual laws are gradually being ignored or discarded, leaving only the core of Judaism - its code of ethics, morality and justice.

Through the ages, the Jews successively introduced such concepts as prayer, church, redemption, universal education, charity; and they did so hundreds of years before the rest of the world was ready to accept them. Is it any wonder that historians credit them as a foundation for much of modern religion.

By the time I graduated from high school, I had never laid eyes on a Jew; they did not exist in our small South Dakota towns. The image of Shylock in Shakespeare's, *The Merchant of Venice*, provided us with a look at the Jewish people; and in Christian Sunday sermons, I heard the Jews were those people who had crucified our Christian Christ. (It did not occur to us that Christ was also a Jew and even a Rabbi of the Jewish Faith). Perhaps some prejudice or a bit jaundiced? Off to college, and I soon found myself with a Jewish roommate. We became close friends and spent many weekends with his family at their home in Denver. I came to a great revelation: Jews are normal people. Unshackling me from some of those racial and religious prejudices was an important part of my college education. We each inherit our culture and traditions, those beliefs, religious faith, and customs that start us on our life. Sometimes that baggage we started life with is in need of change.

3
MY JEWISH FENCE LINES

By Rabbi Paul Gordon

Bernie talks about riding the fence lines that marked the boundaries of his Dakota ranch, and equated that with people of faith who patrol the margins of their ethical and spiritual territory. That is, indeed, an apt description for people in most religions, including my own. Within Judaism we also have inner fence lines that define various movements such as "Conservative", "Reformed", and multiple forms of "Orthodox", each of which differ in some respect. Some things in Judaism are binding for all, while other things can vary. We have two traditions of law. The first are those ethical commandments that we have always considered binding for everyone. The second deal with ritual and traditions that can vary, and in fact, do vary among the different streams of Judaism. You may become confused when I tell you I came in my childhood as a member of a "Reformist" Jewish family, then as I grew to manhood I found myself in college as an "Orthodox" Jew, then later as "Conservative", and now I call myself a "reform-conserv-oxdy" Jew, a hybrid of several streams of Judaism: Reformed, Conservative, and Orthodox.

Let me start with the culture of my youth. I was born in 1970 in Toronto, Canada. We were a traditional nuclear family with a strong and somewhat doctrinaire father who was clearly head of the family, a warm and caring mother, and two brothers and two sisters. While there had not been a rabbi in our family for four generations, religion was always a central part of our culture, and our existence consisted of home, family, and the synagogue. There were no detracting factors I ever encountered that I can recall. Our family were "Reformed" Jews, and the liturgy and prayers we observed in our Toronto environment were comfortable and as much a part of normal life as breathing. A Reformed Jew in the Canada of 1970 is perhaps equivalent to a modern Conservative Jew today in the U.S. They tended to be egalitarian, which is a social philosophy advocating the removal of inequalities among people. When I was a youngster in Canada, women rabbis were starting to be ordained. The way things are done today in the conservative movement in the U.S. is about how things were being done in the Canadian movement 30 years ago.

Even in junior high I was active Jewishly. I studied for my Bar Mitzvah, and there was a youth club called MaccaBee Club, named for the great fighters of the Hasmonean story. We would meet weekly with one of the teachers and I became active in Jewish youth groups.

At the age of 15 when I was about to become confirmed, I became an immigrant when my family moved to San Diego. Talk about cultural shock. Not only did we trade the cold winters of Toronto for the sunny clime of California, we also found a somewhat different stream of Judaism in the Reform synagogue. The north county of San Diego has a very small Jewish community. We attended a public high school and had to travel down to the city of San Diego several nights each week for a supplemental education in a Jewish Hebrew high school. So I was associated with Temple Emanuel in San Diego instead of Temple Emanuel in Toronto, different places, different rabbis, so I had both perspectives which were interesting and meaningful.

With the shock of the move, I postponed my confirmation for a year. Confirmation is the time when a person truly becomes an adult and must re-affirm for himself a religious faith. The catch is, during that year when I re-studied for confirmation, I learned about myself in a different kind of way. We studied the prophets, ethics, values, morals, and I discovered something about myself: there was a passion for belief in law and being Jewish. Now while there was a passion for Judaism, it wasn't necessarily as a rabbi. There were rabbis in my family four generations back, but none since. I am the first in four generations.

Movements within Judaism (The fence lines):

In modern times we talk about the movements, the various streams of Judaism. We avoid the word denomination, because that tends to reflect more changes of theology in the Christian world than how the Jewish world sees itself. The different labels are more based on how we see the law. The force of law within Judaism: where does it have power, and where does it not have power. In other works, what commandments are binding, and which are not. In every single movement there is a strong binding nature of all the ethical commandments. Where we begin to see the big differences is in what we call the ritual commandments. In America, we've got Reform, Reconstructionist, Renewal, Conservative, and multiple forms of Orthodoxy. Within the Orthodox movement there is only one monolithic world, but the traditional Jewish perspective is made up of multiple parts. The most identifiable Orthodox are probably the Hasidic Jews that come from various backgrounds in Eastern Europe that we always see in black hats, long beards, and black coats, all those things in the picture you see when you go to New York City like in the diamond district.

As a broad generalization, Conservative Judaism strikes a middle road between Reform and Orthodox Judaism. For example, unlike Reform, Conservative considers itself bound by almost all Torah rituals as well as Torah ethics. Unlike Orthodox, it considers itself free to introduce innovation in Jewish laws.

But the reality comes back to what is the difference in all these movements in understanding our religion. Judaism is completely different than that of 200 years ago, and in many ways it is the same. We adapt with the times. It is a living tradition. It is not locked into one way of doing things. That has always been one of the strengths about Judaism. It is not a monolithic tradition that insists there is only one way to see the world. It adapts

21

to geographic and regional differences and the theologies that it encounters. There are some basic theologies that always stay constant, such as the belief in one God, the value of Torah (the five Books of Moses), the value of community, the *minyan* as we call it. The *minyan* has a strength that can't be lost, whereas individuals struggling by themselves have a harder time sometimes coming together. So that is a brief background of the movements.

Now having talked about the different streams of Judaism, where would I place myself? Well, you will find that I traveled a circuitous and sometimes tortuous path down these pathways during my youth. When I was in college people started asking me what sort of Jew I was. And the answer I came up with was a "Reform-conserv-odxy" Jew. It is someone who says, you know what, there are valuable parts of Jewish tradition in each of the movements, and I don't like being labeled. A label is a convenient way to say this is what I do or don't do. So a lot of people call themselves a Reform Jew if they don't follow most of the ritual commandments. A lot of people call themselves a Conservative Jew if they follow some of the commandments with respect to ritual, but not all of them. A lot of people call themselves an Orthodox Jew if they follow a lot of the traditional laws; keep the Sabbath, those kinds of things in whatever way they are keeping the Sabbath. When it comes down to trying to label yourself though, it doesn't necessarily describe the theology the person has on the beliefs behind why they do certain things. Some may identify themselves as Orthodox and have the theology of a Reform Jew for all we know, or identify as a Reform Jew and have very traditional ethical beliefs. It is very difficult to try and pigeon-hole people. It is not as simple as within the Protestant world where we say someone is Episcopal and that means something very specific within their belief structure. On somebody is Methodist or Baptist, and that represents a certain set of beliefs. In Judaism there is no one word to describe a Jew, except for the fact they are Jewish.

As I've said, I was raised as a Reform Jew. So that means something very specific in terms of teaching of ethics, teaching of the beliefs from the prophets, and I was raised much more with the ethics and motives behind methodology instead of huge amounts of the tradition of methodology, which are the traditional observances. However, when I was in college I became Orthodox. So it was kind of an interesting dichotomy, going from Reform to Orthodox traditions is like the different ends of the poles. I'm on one pole and all of a sudden I am shifted to the opposite pole. To say my parents were a bit "phased out" when they heard about it, wow! They even came up to college to visit with the Orthodox rabbi who was my teacher at the time to make sure I was okay, and I wasn't going off the edge.

In my family it was a given that I would go to college. I chose California State Northridge, which interesting enough has one of the largest Jewish student populations in the Western United States. It is in the San Fernando Valley, which is about one-quarter Jewish. So there is a high concentration of Jews there, which is one of the reasons I choose the college. The other reason was because they had an excellent music department. When I started college it was my intention to become a professional musician. I was active in music in high school, in the marching band, in concert; I played jazz, all sorts of things. I was a singer. One day a man came to our high school from the Northridge music program and talked about all the opportunities there. They have one of the best music programs in the country, and I was very interested in a career as a musician. But while still a senior in high school, I discovered something else in myself as well: while I love music, I love the challenge, thought, and provoking arguments much more than I did the music. The music was important, but not enough to be my future. So at Northridge I had several other options available for a college education. I liked accounting. I loved the law, I had a potential for business, and all these where there was also a large Jewish population, all in one place. So you know what, it sounded like a place for me.

Like many college freshmen, I became a little confused with questions of doubt about my religious beliefs. So I challenged myself. I took a Jewish studies class, and decided to explore my traditions and heritage. I was still with an undeclared major, hoping to get into a business program, science maybe, a tax attorney, maybe into law school, lots of possibilities.

Then I became involved with a club call the Young Israel, the Orthodoxy Synagogue of God. This Young Israel turned out to be a wonderful place for me. Not only do I become involved with them, and become Orthodox, I also become the *shorshin*, which is kind of like the caretaker for a synagogue. I even lived in the synagogue for two and a half years, and it was a very healthy and good experience for me. It helped to give me discipline and focus. But I was not yet really sure what I wanted to do as a career.

Even before I knew what my major was, I decided on a minor in Jewish studies. This meant taking a dozen classes in Judaism. Still struggling with my career decision, I started thinking, you know, this Jewish studies isn't such a bad thing, so I declared my major in religious studies. In my college education I learned about all religions, not just Judaism. I studied Buddhism, Christianity, Hinduism, and a sense of cultural understanding of religion versus an understanding of religion that was faith based.

Still I struggled with a career decision, because you have to be practical in deciding what you are going to do to make a living. I was thinking of an MBA for business, or maybe going on for a PhD.

I was also having a bit of trouble in my studies and my Orthodox faith. It bothered me that my mother, sisters, and others were excluded from certain positions in Orthodoxy. The position is very limited. They can't come up during a service and read from the Torah, they are specifically given only certain roles in the tradition, perhaps not too meaningful to those people who practice Judaism. I wasn't raised with such restrictions in my earlier tradition, and a little voice in the back of my head began to challenge the thing called equality, an equal voice for all. Egalitarian was important to me.

I considered becoming a cantor, which would further my interest in music, and I looked into cantor role schools, but then decided I had a stronger interest in the rhetorical. Catch me at our Friday night service in the synagogue and you will find me leading the service and participating in the music and sharing that part of me, but it is only part of me, and I was not to be a cantor. Gradually, I began thinking about becoming a rabbi.

So trying to label myself is very difficult if not impossible. You can describe your level of observance maybe, but can't really describe who you are as a person in terms of your beliefs, because beliefs in Judaism are so broad. There are always so many explanations to even the simplest depressions. Let me give you an example. The most visible impression of a Jewish wedding is the breaking of the glass. What is the meaning or symbolism of this tradition. Let me give you three different answers. One, it is to remind us of the sadness of the destruction of the temple in Jerusalem, so we should always remember there is a little sadness at even the most joyous of times. Two, after the glass is shattered into the many thousands of pieces, it should take as many days to put it back together again as the bride and groom will have together. Three, another tradition is a reminder of the fragility of the bonds of marriage, a gift from God, and we must work to keep together otherwise they will end up like the shattered glass. So we have lots of differing explanations within Judaism for this simple tradition. You can imagine how this goes with the more complex theological argument found with the more complex law. This means to be Jewish, you have to be somewhat of a scholar whether you are a rabbi or a lay person.

The reality is to be an active Jew who is practicing both religiously as well as culturally. In Judaism it is very easy to be not practicing religiously and be very strong culturally. To be a really active participant requires that you take the time to study, that you take the time to reflect, take the time to consider what you believe in what you do, why you do it. It is not enough sometimes to say, "Well, this is what God said to do." When it comes down to the basics, then of course that is right. The Ten Commandments set out a clear ethical contract that most communities in the Western World follow to this day. But by the same token, we must look beyond what we call the simple level of knowledge to other traditions contained in such things as we call the interpretive level.

There is more than one way of understanding something. A good example is the translation of one of the Ten Commandments, which is "Thou shall not murder", which is the direct Hebrew translation. In a lot of present day translations this becomes "Thou shall not kill". To kill and murder are very different things. The problem is a lot of the translations were not directly from Hebrew to English, and a lot of the renderings we think of here in America are based on the King James Text. Many modern day translations have modernized the language and don't go back to the original text. There are some texts such as the New International version of the Revised Standard that do go back and revise the text again.

A Rabbi?

So in my senior year of college I decided to become a rabbi. After graduation I applied to JTS, Jewish Theological Seminary in Los Angeles, which is the principal Conservative seminary. It was not an easy decision why I would go there as opposed to an Orthodox rabbinate. For me, the basic question became egalitarian; making sure women and men both had equal voices. Coming out of the Orthodox college background and years of living in their synagogue, a decision to become a Conservative rabbi rather than Orthodox was a stretch. I sorted it out. I have two sisters, a mom, grandmother, all sorts of people who were as important to me as the male side, and I couldn't see practicing in the community if I were not able to administer to them as much as males. So to me, that was one of the driving forces. Admission was not easy and took months of preparation. I had to write detailed essays, and do whole reflections study on myself. I had to go through a psychological review. They wanted to make sure I was a nice, stable guy. I was admitted, and at the age of 22 I was loving everything.

Yet, from the time I got there I was troubled by some of the things they were doing. While the conservative movement is a centralist movement within Judaism that believes much more in the force of law than Reform in terms of the ritual, it still did not quite satisfy me. I also had a few issues and problems with some of the administrators and academic officers, and I questioned some things, and they don't always like it if you don't question things in just the right way. So after two years I left the Jewish Theological Seminary, and transferred to a school called the Academy for Jewish Religion, AJR, located in New York City. It was the only pluralistic seminary in the United States. It has teachers who are Orthodox, Conservative, Reform, Reconstructionalist, and Jewish Renewal. They pull from the best of everybody. So I moved to New York, and spent five years studying there. During those years I learned how to be a rabbi not only for conservative Jews, but for all Jews. And to me, as I said at the very beginning, I consider myself a Reform-Conserv-Oxdy Jew.

The process in which you become a rabbi is a bit different than in the Christian community where you are ordained by the community that you go to. In Judaism, ordination is given by a group of rabbis. If you look at my ordination certificate, it has numerous rabbi signatures. Let me translate into English the text of the certificate, which will give you a sense of what it means to be a rabbi.

> **"We the undersigned standards, teachers, and members of the Board of Trustees do hereby certify that Paul Gordon has completed the required studies and Bible liturgy, rabbinic law and law, philosophy, history, is prepared spiritually and professionally to meet the Jewish people. Accordingly we resolve to grant you to serve as Rabbi and Teacher in Israel. To bring honor, to bring joy to the House of Israel, to increase peace in the world, may his life be fulfilled, and may God be with you always."**

I was ordained in New York City at the Society for the Advance of Judaism, which is one of the oldest liberal synagogues in the United States? I have officially been a rabbi now for three years, but I have been practicing in the field a lot longer than I have been ordained. While I was in school I felt I needed to get out in the field for some professional development, so as a student rabbi I was in New Hampshire for three years in a small synagogue of Hasidic families. They called me rabbi, and I worked at it, but I did not claim the title for myself because I was not yet ordained. While I work at a conservative school here in Modesto, it is the only synagogue in the area and has a diverse population that included not only Conservative, but those from other movements. I have some Jews who are traditional and would go to an Orthodox synagogue if there were one, and I have some Jews who are much more liberal and come here because it is the only game in town, otherwise they would go to a Reform synagogue. I have some people who are interested in spirituality who would go to a Renewal synagogue if there were one. But they are all under the same roof.

So the variety within the membership of my eclectic synagogue dictates a lot of my approaches. The way I do services here is different than in a synagogue without such a diverse population. Friday nights I do a more liberal service than I do on Saturday morning, so that way you know if you are more liberal to come on Friday night, and more traditional to come on Saturday morning. That way, everybody has a place they can come and pray. It is important to give everyone a voice. That is why we do different kinds of service. We do a family service to make sure younger families have a place they can bring their kids. We do all sorts of different things to help make this a meaningful and vibrant community.

Much of my time as a rabbi is devoted to the life-cycle basics that all clergy of any faith are involved in such as birth, marriage, and death. Shortly after coming to this synagogue we had a rash of 15 people who died in the first year I was here. Then in the Jewish faith our time also includes baby names, circumcism for a Jewish boy, Bar and Bat Mitzvah for young people when they are 12 or 13 years of age, and confirmation when they are 16 years of age. Then of course, a major portion of my time is spent on sturdy, teaching, and providing leadership to the Beth Shalom congregation.

Unlike the structure of many other religious groups, there is no hierarchy in the rabbinate. There are a few rabbinic groups in the United States, but there is no one overall chief rabbi here in the U.S. In Israel there is a chief rabbi and he is appointed by the government. In England there is a chief rabbi, and he is appointed by the government.

In some ways, each rabbi is responsible more of less to himself or herself as the deciding authority and for rabbi commentaries, because there are various specialized skills. That is why a rabbi must spend so much time in study. Just because a rabbi is trained to read Hebrew doesn't mean they can work with any kind of community.

The way it works in the United States is we work on a congregational basis, similar in some ways to the more liberal way in some Christian denominations which do not have a hierarchy. When a synagogue needs to hire a rabbi, they go through a search process by contacting various rabbinical organizations. Those groups will filter the right kind of rabbi to the right group. There is a shortage of rabbi in this country at the present time. Of the entire rabbis who get ordained, only about 50% actually choose to go into a congregational rabbinate. That is a nice thing about the rabbinate, that you are not locked into community work. You could go to a Jewish federation, community rabbi position, work as a chaplain, work in hospitals, prisons, military chaplains, work as a scholar, or work on a college campus. There are rabbis who work with a number of major Catholic universities who want to have someone on staffs who is an expert on rabbinate law, because people do still learn about those things.

Hebrew and prayer:

While English is my first and principle language, Hebrew is the language of the Judaic religion. I learned Hebrew as a young person how to read it, but I did not really learn it as a language until I got to college at Northview, as an academic study. I had learned it in bits and pieces, but not with the ability to have a conversation or to study text in detail.

For Jews, the Sabbath begins on Friday night. Why Friday night? In the very beginning of Geneses you read, "In the first day of creation, the day was created and there was evening and there was morning the first day." So since it says evening first, by Jewish tradition, we dictate the day actually starts in the evening prior. So that is why our Sabbath and holidays start the prior evening.

A Jew must pray three times each day, the morning prayer is the *Shakharit*, the afternoon is the *Minkha*, and the evening prayer is *Ma'ariv*. The evening prayer on Friday is a bit different. It has two main sections, the *Cololot* and the *Ma'ariv*. The *Cololot* is the acceptance of receiving of the Sabbath, and it is a tradition that began in a little town in northern Israel about 400 years ago, and has become universally accepted in the Jewish community. The *Ma'ariv* evening prayer service involves two major sets of prayers. Most are sung or chanted by the community as a whole, and myself as prayer leader. Some are read in English. Sometimes we do creative reading or poetry. Also we have what we call the *abatoruim*, which is like a sermon. Sometime we do the *Kiddush*, which is the sanctification of the Sabbath. We oftentimes use grape juice instead of wine in our service since it is important we have the right social message. We fill the glass up all the way, and if it were wine it could have an effect on driving

So the Friday night service is the beginning of the Sabbath, which is more than just a day of reflection, but a day of rest, and celebration of coming together as a community of families. We have special meals for the Sabbath that we do not have the rest of the week. All sorts of special things happen.

Another language often associated with Jews is Yiddish. It is something I know very little of. Yiddish comes from a combination of Hebrew, German, and a few other European languages, and there are different dialects of it depending on where you are from. If Russian, you have a different dialect than if you were from Poland, and a different dialect than if you were German. While there a lot of similar words in each of the dialects, there are also unique words for each one. I learned Hebrew. I understand four different dialects of Hebrew. It is the main language of Israel now, it is the language of the Torah, it is the language of the commentaries, and the law. So Hebrew is the language a Jew needs.

Judaic literature:

I am sure you are acquainted with the Bible of the Christian faith and the Koran for Muslims. There are comparable books of the Judaic faith, but because of the span of several millenniums during the development of our literature, the story is complex. Let me place these in a historical context.

First came the Torah, which is another name for the Written Law, and it contains the commandments. These are the Five Books of Moses, and they date back at least to the ninth century BCE. Over the early centuries, a legal commentary on the Torah was developed, which explained how its commandments are to be carried out. This oral tradition was needed to accompany the written law as a guide to Jewish life. This oral extension of the Written Law (Torah) resulted in the creation of the Mishna, or Oral Law, and this was finally written down about 186 CE by Rabbi Judah-ha-Nasi, who was head of the Rabbinical High Court, who decided to make sure the oral law and the traditions were not lost.

Then in the third century CE, a large body of commentary was produced which, combined with the Mishna, is known as the Talmud. There are 37 different volumes in the Babylonian Talmud. There is also a Jerusalem Talmud, written simultaneously but in different locations, and the two collections of various rabbinic sources have been placed together into 63 books, called tractates. Each tractate contains both the Mishna and the Gemara, which is a commentary on the Mishna that various rabbis wrote over the centuries. So it is commentary on top of commentary. So these 63 tractates, or volumes, comprise the Talmud. It comprises the entire range of Jewish law, and in addition it contains materials on many other subjects that affect human life. The tractate *Shabbat* contains all the laws pertaining to the Sabbath, *Mishna Brakhot* deals with blessings, *Mishna Nashim* deals with women, *Zera'im* deals with seeds and agrarian laws, etc. So while each rabbi is responsible to his or her self as the deciding authority, within the Talmud they will find certain decisions of the law that they can make for any given situation.

A whole other genre of Jewish literature going beyond the Talmud is the Midrash, which is a style of story telling and legal analysis. Most Jewish literature is trying to fill in the blanks. Where is the story telling you things and what are the blanks? Let me give you an example from Midrash. It tells a story about Abraham, who was the patriarch who started the Hebrews and later the Jews. His father, Terah, was an idol maker in his workshop. Abraham encountered God. He realized God was calling him, and realized there was one Deity, and that Deity did not have a face, and there was not any idol you could make for it. One day when his father left the workshop, the little boy Abraham, not yet eight, smashed all the idols except for one, and he placed a large club in that idols hand. His father returned and saw the horror of all his business idols smashed. Then he saw the idol with the club and asked Abraham what happened. Abraham looked innocently at his father and said the big idol had smashed all the rest. The father replied that was impossible since the idol was only made of stone and can't come to life. Abraham said, "That's true, Father. If he can't come to life, then we know the truth that he is not really God, then why should God allow for any of these idols to be a God?" What is the moral of the story? Abraham realized the nature of God and wanted to teach his father about it. The point of this story from the Midrash is that it was filling in the blanks. You are not going to find this story in the Five Books of Moses, the Torah. It is a legend, a piece of lore that helps explain why Abraham chose God, and why God chose Abraham. There are a lot of these stories in Midrash, and some of them even found their way into the Christian Bible stories. You will find the stylized telling and re-telling of the day, and in parallel with the New Testament that was written in the same time period. A part of the New Testament is actually based on the Jewish Midrash. That is not to say it is not valid material for those people, but only to understand where they drew it from. The New Testament was contemporary writings with the Midrash.

A concluding prayer:

I want to thank Bernie for inviting me to ride the fence lines of my faith with him. As I said previously, Judaism is completely different than that of 200 years ago, and in many ways it is the same. We adapt with the times. It is a living tradition. As a rabbi, a "teacher", I also continue to grow in my religious faith. It has been my pleasure to visit with you and talk about my life as a Jew; first as a youth going through the formulative years, then the years when I struggled in going through the circuitous path exploring issues of faith, and finally my life as I became a rabbi to serve here in the Beth Shalom congregation.

Permit me to conclude with a prayer. This blessing is known in Hebrew as *Birkat Kahanim*, or the priest's blessing. It is a blessing performed near the end of many of our services.

May the Lord bless and protect you.
May the Lord make His face shine upon you and be gracious to you.
May the Lord lift up His countenance upon you and grant you peace.

4

CAMP CROOK

The High Plains, the beginning of the desert west, often act as a crucible for those who inhabit them. Like Jacob's angel, the region requires that you wrestle with it before it bestows a blessing.

When Terah led the Hebrews out of Mesopotamia into the arid Mountains of Turkey, he found desolation like Dakota where I was raised. The little town of Camp Crook is located in one of the most isolated parts of the United States, set apart by distance, topography, and a last-frontier culture of the old west. This was the beginning of my religious culture.

The cowboys who settled the range lands of Montana, Wyoming, and the Dakotas were mostly infidels who had no religious faith, as described by one of them who trailed the herds north:

"…….. That family stuffed me full of all that religious bull when I was a kid, but I never had any more use for it after I was growed, and in that I was like the rest of the cowpunchers. Ninety per cent of them were infidels."

The bulk of them were confederates mustered out at the end of the Civil War who drifted to Texas, found a depression there, and joined the cattle herds moving north. After the herds reached their northern terminus, the cowboys with no place better to go often stayed and settled on small claims in this wild country which still had wandering bands of the Sioux, Cheyenne, and Crow. Since they lived in isolation on the prairie far from any church, an organized religion played no part in their existence. The few traces of Christianity that later reached these northern plains came with the women who found their way north and became spouses. But despite the absence of a church, these people who shared a hard way of life, dependent on each other for security and substance, displayed a life style more in keeping with Christian ways than many of those in the "civilized east" who went to church every Sunday. They knew the difference between right and wrong and didn't need a preacher to tell them that.

Camp Crook was a frontier town located in this desolate country in northwest South Dakota on the Montana border. Like many other frontier settlements, it has been a ghost town now for sixty years; some say it was never much different since it's birth when General Crook, the Sioux Indian fighter, camped there and bestowed his name on the tumbleweeds and baked mud bluffs alongside the Little Missouri River. Not that I recall much about Camp Crook; we left during the thirties depression when nearly everyone else did, and moved away. I returned last summer for a look in at my ancestral home and found only a few tumble-down, vacant buildings that line a dirt street, a house or two that gave the appearance that someone still lived there, and a barking dog that greeted the car as we passed by.

I was surprised to find an abandoned building with a steeple and cross that identified it as a church, as I could not recall ever having been in a church in Camp Crook. During the years we lived there, the only priest or ministers we ever saw were traveling missionaries who came through sporadically. I was baptized by a missionary priest in our house during the cold month of February when no parishioner could be coaxed into a frigid church. At that stage in their lives, my parents were not much for church going. My father, Catholic in name, had been raised by his widowed father at Cuyahoga, a gold mine camp in the Black Hills. It was a seven mile ride on horseback to the nearest church in Custer, and that trip was made only on rare occasions. My mother was raised in a rigid Methodist environment that forbade dancing and card playing, which she ignored as much a possible during her teen years; and was happy to enter a mixed marriage, where organized religion was placed on a back burner. Immediately after they were married, they moved to Camp Crook to live in the land of infidels,

36

and their Christianity was simplified to the basics of treating each other and their neighbors with kindness and following the Ten Commandments. My parents were wonderful role models; with grace and little fanfare they brought a religious spirit into our lives with what they said and did.

Building churches in Camp Crook was a chancy enterprise with sporadic and shifting religious interest and few resources. Early religious services were held in homes, organized by the few women-folk who came with a religious upbringing from elsewhere. The first endeavor to build a church, twenty six years after the town was first settled, was by the Methodist. A traveling minister attempted to organize a fund raising campaign, but the project came to a standstill for lack of funds. An attempt to convert it to a Union church also failed. Later the Baptist took over the project and completed the church with a gift of money from a parish in Pennsylvania; ten years later the church was closed for lack of parishioners. A new effort by the Methodist to raise funds was successful, and the church was purchased to become a Methodist church. It remained an active parish for five decades, but is now opened only on special occasions when a traveling minister is in the area.   A Seventh Day Adventist Church was formed by a small group who built a church that remained open for three decades, but was closed for lack of parishioners. A Catholic church was built, but a priest was seldom assigned to the parish, and the building has been abandoned.

Another "religious" fringe group operated in the shadows, although factual history is difficult to establish. This was the Ku Klux Klan group that existed in Camp Crook during the 1920's. They were a secret group that conducted an occasional cross burning alongside the river. Who belonged to the group was never openly proclaimed, but it was rumored they were bootleggers who operated stills in the isolated parts of the Little Missouri Valley. This was the era of social change involving prohibition, temperance movements, women's rights, anti-immigrant campaigns, emerging ethnic and racial tensions; feelings ran strong for and against various elements of society. The motive force for this KKK clan was unclear since there was not a single Negro living within hundreds of miles; apparently it was just a hell-raising group of infidels who wanted to express a symbolic gesture against social change - particularly against the temperance movement. Who knows? Today, we'd probably dismiss them as local "red necks".

When I drove through Camp Crook last year, there was one establishment still open called a general store. It occupied the dilapidated building that had been my father's bank. Behind the counter was an iron door leading into the old vault with the inscription still legible, "LITTLE MISSOURI BANK", now a storeroom full of canned goods. A young girl tended the counter. I tried to recall a few names from the past with her, but there was no sign of recognition, and she expressed little interest in the history of the place. As I headed out of town, I wondered if I should have come back. Maybe it is best to let the ghosts from your childhood lie in peace.

5

BUDDHISM

"A religion originated in India by Gautama Buddha five centuries before Christ and later spreading to China, Burma, Japan, Tibet, and parts of southeast Asia, holding that life is full of suffering caused by desire and that the way to end this suffering is through enlightenment that enables one to halt the endless sequence of births and deaths to which one is otherwise subject."

If any religion would appeal to an infidel cowboy, the one coming closest might be Buddhism. Cowboys spend a lot of time alone in contemplation, commune with their spirits, and live in a near-monastic world with few boundaries. Buddhism is so loosely defined that it can be embraced by almost anyone; there are few fence lines to hem one in; yes, it fits a cowboy's style. The founder of the Buddhist religion, Gautama, founded a religion twenty-six centuries ago that is still embraced by some of the world's largest populations. What is the pull of this simple religion?

Some of my friends think I'm religious, while others suspect I am a closet infidel. I am not sure which is accurate, but I have developed considerable tolerance for all religious faiths, even for agnostics who think it is all "pie in the sky". Some of this developed because of travel around the world where I witnessed people of different cultures who were sincere in their own religious beliefs. I began to wonder if any one culture had a sole ownership of a one, true faith. Buddhism is a case at point; if I were not already Catholic, I think I might be Buddhist - perhaps our closest relative with its meditation, prayer, chanting, and that wonderful place of Nirvana.

Small wonder that this ancient religion has such an appeal to young Americans, and is a church with growing membership in our country.

Here is some powerful stuff that was authored five hundred years before Christ - long before the Greeks, Romans, or Western Civilization - by a guy called Buddha.

* All the miseries and discontent of life can be traced to selfishness.
* Suffering is due to the craving individuality, to the torment
   of greedy desire.
* Until man overcomes every sort of personal craving his life is
   trouble, and his end sorrow.
* The three forms of craving in life are:
   To gratify the senses.
   For personal immorality.
   Desire for prosperity, worldliness.
* All these must be overcome. When they are and no longer rule a man's
   life, then he has reached the higher Wisdom, Nirvana, serenity of soul.

My first encounter with the Buddhist religion was in Japan, although there it is called Shinto. I was in the navy during the Korean War and saw statues of Budda all over the orient. The religion seemed mysterious. An important development in my education came many years later when a daughter became an AFS exchange student and lived with a Buddhist family in Thailand. She returned home with great affection for these people and respect for their religion, which she explained was compatible with her Catholic faith. This opened my eyes, and during my subsequent business travels through the Buddhist countries of China, Japan, Thailand, and Taiwan, I was able to accept these people and their religion at face value. I was surprised with some similarities to my Christian faith, and some interesting parallels in the life of Budda with two prophets who were to come later, Jesus Christ and Mohammed.

Six hundred years before the time of Christ, when the Babylon Empire flourished in the Near East, there was another civilization in far away India. This peninsula was an enclave, locked by the Himalayas Mountains that cut off ties to the north, and the seas on the other three sides, so there were few ties elsewhere. Within India a tranquil life had survived for centuries. "The nobleman, the rajahs, hunted; life was made up of love stories. Here and there a maharajah arose amidst the rajahs and built a city, caught and tamed many elephants, slew many tigers, and left a tradition of his splendor and his wonderful possessions".

It was during this time that Gautama, the founder of Buddhism was born. He was a young man of fortune, born into an aristocratic life, and at the age of nineteen he married a beautiful lady, his cousin. For many years they remained childless. During this time he grew restless, and despaired of the idle and meaningless aristocratic life of endless pleasure. He began to have visions of another world, one that included disease, distress, and misery.

When he was twenty nine, his wife delivered his first-born son. On that night, he awoke in a great agony of spirit. He went softly to the threshold of his wife's chamber, where he saw her sleeping, holding his child in her arms. He turned, walked into the bright moon light, mounted a horse, and rode away into another world, never to return.

Making his way southward to another region of India, he joined a resort of hermits and teachers who lived in a warren of caves. Their discussions were similar to those of Socrates, who was to live in the Greek culture three centuries later. With the mind of a genus, Gautama became versed in all the metaphysics of his age, but he became dissatisfied with the solution to life he found offered amongst the hermits; so he left, taking with him five disciples and fled to the jungle. He gave himself up to fasting, self-mortification, and terrible penance until one day he staggered and fell unconscious. When he recovered, he changed his life-style to one that emphasized a nourished brain in a well-fed and healthy body. Then he left his disciples and wandered alone through India, a lonely figure, searching for the light of knowledge. At long last, he again sought out his five disciples. They now hailed him as the Buddha. There was, already in those days, a belief in India that at long intervals Wisdom returned to the earth and was revealed to mankind through a chosen person known as the Buddha. According to the Indian belief there have been many such Buddha, and Gautama was only the latest one of a series, but the unpretentious Gautama never called himself the Buddha.

With his disciples he formed an academy, and their fame spread by word of mouth; at that time there was as yet no writing in India. His essential doctrines, that were listed earlier, address some of the basic tenants that will reappear in other religions. All these personal cravings of man must be overcome. When they are and no longer rule a man's life, he has reached the higher Wisdom, Nirvana, serenity of soul. Nirvana is not a place or a thing; it is a state of mind, and when man reaches this higher plateau, he is freed from the base cravings that otherwise rule a man's life. It is in Nirvana where man loses himself in something greater than himself. Centuries later the Bible was to say, "Whosoever would save his life, shall lose it" - essentially the same lesson.

In the teaching of Buddha there is no social order, no security, no peace or happiness, no righteous leadership or kingship, unless man loses himself in something greater than himself. There was no Buddhist church, mosque, or temple in the days of Gautama. The Buddha was silent on such questions as the creation of the universe, the existence of God, and the nature of an afterlife. In their tradition, these are the great silences. The primary exercise is self-examination, to know the self, and to see that nothing is forever.

Buddhism differed from all the other religions of its day. "It was primarily a religion of conduct, not a religion of observances and sacrifices. It has no temples; and, since it had no sacrifices, it had no sacred order of priests. Nor had it any theology. It neither asserted nor denied the reality of the many Gods who were worshipped in India or elsewhere at the time: It passed them by." All of this was six centuries before the time of Christ, and a thousand years before Muhammad.

In almost all religions some changes or revisions develop over time. It was the fate of Gautama that some disciples, in their efforts to impress others in the outer world, made him into a Wonder. While he saw himself as a teacher, they sold him as a near God. Buddhism also became constrained by the ingrown nature of Indian life where there was little sense of history, and the cycle of life kept repeating over and over. This lead to a doctrine of "Karma", in which the good or evil of every life was supposed to determine the happiness or misery of some subsequent life that was in some inexplicable way identified with its predecessor. The Indian mind in their confined society was full of the idea of cyclic recurrence; everything was supposed to come around again. That concept was not central to the teachings of Gautama, but it gradually became an appendage added to his religion by others, the doctrine of reincarnation. This doctrine as it gradually developed taught that those who follow the Buddha way in their life will be reincarnated as a more enlightened person. Eventually a person may enter into a different state of being in the Heavens.

Buddhism made its way into central Asia through Afghanistan and Turkistan, traveling with the Grand Lamas who wore special robes on their journeys and performed ceremonies in their temples involving benediction with a blessing by laying hands on the heads of the faithful, spiritual retreats, the worship of saints, fasting, processions, litanies, holy water, and other religious acts that were to be repeated in other religions in the centuries to come. It reached China about AD 64. "There it found a popular religion already established, Taoism, a development of very ancient and primitive magic and occult practices. Tao means The Way. The two religions spread side by side, underwent similar changes, and nowadays their outward practice is very similar." In China, Buddhism also encountered Confucianism, which was less theoretical and more a code of personal conduct. Confucius lived in China during the sixth century BC, just prior to the time of Gautama in India. He was of aristocratic birth, and after occupying various official positions, he set up an academy for the discovery and imparting of wisdom. His teachings centered upon the idea of a noble life which he embodies in a standard or ideal, the Aristocratic Man. The Chinese speak of Buddhism, the doctrines of Lao Tse (Taoism), and Confucius as the Three Teachings. Together they constitute the basis and point of departure of all later Chinese thought.

The religion gradually spread to Japan where it found the Shinto cult already in existence and gradually over-shadowed it, but several centuries later the doctrines were combined. Today it is essentially the Buddhist doctrine but with the name of Shinto. During my time in Japan I often visited the Shinto temples to sit in quiet meditation. Their large open space with few adornments was not intimidating and offered an ideal place to collect one's thoughts.

Gautama was openly against the caste system of ancient India, and for that reason Buddhist were a threat to the Brahmins, the higher intelligential caste. It was this Brahmins caste group that eventually was able to oust Buddhism from India, the land of its origin; so this religion no longer exists in India, the place where it started.

Today, Buddhism is the dominate religion of Asia. There are an estimated 340 million Buddhist worldwide, and 600,000 in North America. It has two broad divisions. Southern Buddhism, called Hinayana, in India, Burma, Cambodia, and Thailand is the more traditional and smaller branch, and is linked to a monastic lifestyle, renunciation of the world, and pursuit of enlightenment. Northern Buddhism, called Mahayana, in China, Korea, and Japan is more geared to the lay person; it relates religion to life in the world and promotes interaction among believers to attain enlightenment. Besides these there are Lamaism in Tibet and Mongolia, which are a mixture of Mahayana Buddhism and the Animistic Bon religion of Tibet. As with Christianity and Islam, both of which manifest themselves through many different systems, Buddhism has evolved into this multitude of expressions. The variety comes not only from the natural doctrinal differences that sprout within any religion, but from Buddhism's inherent tolerance which allows devotees to incorporate elements of other religions such as Christianity into their individual practice.

For several centuries after the death of Buddha, the scriptural traditions were transmitted orally. These were finally committed to writing about the first century BC in Sanskrit. Today, these writings are known generally as the Sutra, a collection of precepts, and a discourse of the Buddha. It can be compared to the Bible of Christians, Koran of Muslims, and Talmud of the Jews.

If you were to visit a typical Buddhist center in America, what might you see? Your first impression would be of absolute quiet in a sparsely furnished, carpeted room. A Buddhist minister or nun sitting on the carpet leads meditation. An altar bearing apples, oranges, flowers, water, and a bell rests before a painting of Buddha. It is not for worship; the image is to remind us of human potential. Such quiet moments of contemplation are reflected in elements of Zen and yoga meditation, not only to stretch their bodies and relax their minds, but also to explore the spiritual dimensions of the soul.

Regardless of our own personal religion, perhaps we could all use a bit of that quiet meditation that Buddhist do so well. A cowboy infidel, working by himself on the prairie and spending nights alone watching the campfire embers die, can relate to the quiet contemplation of Buddhism. Riding those fence lines is familiar territory.

6

I AM A BUDDHIST MINISTER

By Dr. Seigen Yamaoka

At the conclusion of his chapter, Bernie Keating said he could relate to Buddhism because of his life as a cowboy on the prairie of Dakota: alone, lost in his thoughts while watching the campfire embers die. That is probably true. Quiet meditation is certainly a central aspect of my life as a Buddhist.

Bernie also talks about the fences on his ranch domain that kept their stock in and other stock out, and compares this with the boundaries man uses to define their particular religious faith. This parody is somewhat appropriate, although in Buddhism our boundaries are so obscure they may compare more with open range.

Like so many others, my religious faith was shaped by the environment into which I was born and raised. I was born in Fresno, California to immigrant parents who worked the land. My parents were Buddhists. Due to the advent of World War II and life in camps during the war, I was not active in the Japanese and Buddhist communities. The reason being, both emphasized my Japanese side, which was constantly being challenged. To find my place, I had to do a lot of fighting. In my college years, I became more involved with the Japanese and Buddhist communities because they had a basketball league. In time, I was asked to be president of a new local

Young Buddhist Association. Because of my activities, a cousin suggested I consider ministry. I did not feel qualified, so I rejected the idea. My cousin's insistence became public knowledge and soon I found myself being swept into ministry, but I did not resist.

Ministry does have its ups and downs, but because of ministry I am able to share all aspects of life with people and find myself learning from each event and the truth of Buddhism in its daily application.

In general the style in the chapter Bernie wrote about Buddhism is fine; however, we need to express some points to clarify why Buddhism is a universal teaching.

Guatama (Siddhartha), upon leaving the four gates, realized that there was suffering in the world. Yet, he did not understand the cause of suffering even though he was in the midst of it.

Upon attaining enlightenment, he realized that all things were dependently originated, that is, all things are interrelated, but in a process of constant change. Nothing was outside of this fundamental truth of the universe. He had come to see the cause of suffering!

Therefore in the Four Truth he states that (1) Life is suffering because we are unable to understand the significance of interrelationships and change. (2) We are ignorant of the truth and are attached to things that change. Hence, we suffer. (3) We must rid ourselves of our attachment and ignorance. (4) The way is the Eightfold Path, which is right view, thought, speech, conduct, livelihood, effort, mindfulness, and meditation. If we are able to view all things as interrelated and changing and live accordingly, we come to the realization of the truth of life.

The application of this truth is universal to everyone and to all beings. Yet, the application of this truth is personal because we will experience its meaning in our own unique way. Thus, the Buddha preached to all persons depending on the capability and capacity. His teachings remain for monks and laypersons or householders alike.

Thus, in Buddhism there are two basic streams. They are Buddhism for the monks and Buddhism for the householders. Buddhism for the monks is a teaching in which the disciples emulate the historical Buddha's drive to attain enlightenment. Buddhism for the householder is the teaching in which the person cannot emulate the historical Buddha's drive to attain enlightenment. The Buddha, moved by his compassionate enlightenment, revealed the way by which enlightenment-truth moves toward such persons and awakens the truth in them.

Many people refer to Gautama as the one and only Buddha, however that is not entirely correct. While the Indian religious leader, Gautama, was Buddha and founder of Buddhism, the term refers to any of a series of teachers, of whom Gautama was the last. Buddha is actually a title or designation of one who has awakened to the universal truth of life and the world within which we live. Buddha, being awakened to the truth of life, shares the truth with all beings so they can find truth for themselves. He is not a creator. He works with the issue of suffering and how to become aware of the cause for suffering and find meaning.

Many other religions have some sort of central government or unifying structure that guides their doctrines, but Buddhism differs in this respect. In the time of Buddha a unifying structure was not important because of the personalization of self-growth that Buddhism deals with. Its concern is simply to clarify why each person suffers. When each person comes to understand that truth, it is shared with those who have yet to understand. It is this process which gives Buddhism its uniqueness. It can flow and grow with the times and changes because it deals with the flow of changes as a truth.

The encyclopedia refers to Nirvana as a state of mind rather than a place or a thing. In Buddhism, Nirvana is defined in many ways, but in reality it is being one with the universal truth of life. It can be said to be a state of mind as in enlightenment, and it can be said to be that which is truth-itself. This will all become clear as one resolves the issue of life in the flow of life.

Nearly every religion has some historical literature such as the Jewish Talmud, Christian Bible, and the Islamic Koran, and perhaps a comparable literature for Buddhism is the Sutra, which is a collection of aphorisms relating to some aspect of the conduct of life. The Sutra is a collection of the words of the historical Buddha. It can deal with whatever the Buddha felt was important to his listeners at that time. He dealt with many issues of life, interrelationships, practices, way of life, etc. He realized that all persons were different and unique. One thing we must understand is the Sutras are not the end in itself, but a door, which opens other possibilities.

Various religions believe in an afterlife of some form, such as a Christian belief in Heaven and Hell, but the Buddhist faith is silent on this subject. Of course, you must realize that Buddhism existed for a number of centuries before Christianity. The Buddha, depending on the listeners' capability, spoke about a Pure Land of Enlightenment or for the monks taught about the emptiness of all things. But, the fundamental focus was on the issue of life now, and how we understand it. While Reincarnation is associated with Buddhism, it was something he referred to because it came from another tradition, and is not central to the faith. Budda always emphasized that what is important is the now. A now that is constant in the flow of time.

If you were to attend a Buddhist temple and service, and I invite you to do so, you would find some similarities with the Christian church and some differences. Every temple is different based on its unique tradition, however, if you stepped into a Jodo Shinshu or Pure Land Temple in America you will find the setting unique, but the services somewhat similar to the American religious services. One basic difference will be the chanting. The reason for this is that during the early discrimination that was exerted on the Japanese immigrant community any gathering that was different was suspect. Therefore, in order to achieve understanding from the community at large, priests were called Reverends, temples called churches, and services held on Sunday. There are other reasons of course. Anyone is welcomed to attend services. Behavior should be one of learning and growing.

In recent years there has developed a much greater tolerance among many of the religions of the world; if not acceptance of others dogma's and tenants of faith, at least more open lines of communication among religious, often referred to as the new "ecumenical" spirit. Buddhism has always been ecumenical because it does not challenge any belief. Its main concern is the issue of resolving suffering. Therefore, Buddhism is not a threat to any religious tradition. For this reason in Buddhism there is not a heavy emphasis on converting people. We must spend more time on the issue of the truth of suffering. The ecumenical movement is good in this regard.

Budda was a teacher who taught us this message: "The wholeness of our lives can be found in the simple realization that all things in life are interdependent but in the process of change. This is the beginning of all religious life. We need to look at this truth in order to find meaning, value, and responsible respect for all life."

Now we live in a modern world with the internet, and I use Email to communicate with my congregation of the Oakland Buddhist Temple, and each month I provide them with a reflection to help them find meaning and value in their lives. Bernie will include a few from the recent past.

Post script by Bernie: Since meeting Dr Yamaoka, I have been placed on his Email list and each month I receive a short reflection to think about during the month. While they sometimes resemble a message from inside a fortune cookie, I have found these Email reflections make me pause, and they often help place the events of the day in a new light for me. With Dr Yamaoka's permission, I will share those I received within the past year.

Happy New Year. Reflection: In life experiences always remember that there are ups and downs, but they are to be treasured. In the process of life both are important.

January reflection: It is often said that Loves moves the world; which may be true. However it is Gratitude that saves the world.

February reflection: Change is the movement of life in whatever form that it takes. Seeing change as the truth of life is the great challenge of life.
March reflection: We can only see ourselves because we are mirrored and

sustained by the universal interrelationships that surround us.

April reflection: Change is the condition within which the Great Compassions helps us to find meaning for our lives.

May reflection: A question was asked, "What is the meaning of life? Answer, "Live!"

June reflection: We often think that time is passing us by. Yes, time is passing us by until we make something out of that precious time.

July reflection: People say that life is precious! Equally precious is time. We need to take care of both at the same time.

August reflection: People often say that success is the key to life. True, but to find meaning in the "ups" and "downs" that we experience in life is the real key.

9/11/2001 reflection: On this day, in memory for those who lost their lives in the tragic event, let us join the world in expressing our heartfelt thoughts in meditation.

> First, may the Enlightenment-Truth of Wisdom and Compassion, Infinite Light and Life, known to us as Amida, embrace all those who lost their lives in that tragic event and those who are suffering the agonies and uncertainties of having lost loved ones. Second, Let us, who are gathered today, being embraced in the Enlightenment-Truth of Amida, send forth loving thoughts of comfort to all those who feel the pains of this tragic event with the hope that, in time, peace of heart will prevail. Finally, as we move on from this day with varied feelings and thoughts, let us be ever mindful of the words found in the Dharmapada, which says,"Hate is not over come by hatred, hatred is over come by love. This is an ancient rule."

October reflection: Time and life continues to move on. We must reflect within that time and life in order to make our lives meaningful.

November reflection: Joys in life come from many directions, but the meaning of life can come from only one-a self embraced by life.

December reflection: The beauty of life is not how it begins or ends, but how it continues to grow moment to moment.

Take care
Gassho
Seigen Yamaoka

7

BUFFALO GAP

Some towns die, and are dead,
But ours, though it perished, breathes;
And, in old men and in young dreamers
Still, glows and seethes.

In Buffalo Gap I was witness to a change of eras, when the heathen Sioux Indians were driven onto reservations to be replaced on the Dakota plains by white settlers. The Sioux warriors and white settlers co-existed at Buffalo Gap in a tenuous peace, old men who had fought their last battles. Two settlers, Gene Griffis and Bill Sewright, were my neighbors. No-Water, High Eagle, and Black Elk were old warriors who came off the reservation to pitch their teepees alongside the creek across from us, and work on the Sewright ranch to repay their debts for provisions bartered to them the previous winter. While the old warriors seldom spoke to the white man, their grandchildren were my playmates, so they accepted me as one of their own.

We lived in the shadow of the Black Hills, which the Sioux called Paha Sapa. A corridor from the mountains down onto the prairie was called Buffalo Gap, because the buffalo could leave the mountains and reach their winter feeding grounds on the prairie. A little stream flowed from the mountains through this gap and meandered onto the plains, eventually reaching the Cheyenne River. The buffalo herds followed this water trail as they moved back and forth from mountain to prairie, so it was a favorite hunting grounds for the Sioux. Pitching their teepees alongside the stream, they created an Indian village in the fall and spring when buffalo were on the move.

The Indians did not live in the Black Hills because of the frightening presence of thunderclaps, lightening storms, bears, and hostile God-like phenomena they could not control and did not understand. They held these forbidding mountains, Paha Sapa, in reverence, but lived elsewhere on the Great Plains that stretched to the horizon on all sides. The Sioux survived by living off the buffalo herds; they ate the meat, lived in teepees made of buffalo hides, wore buffalo capes against the cold of winter, and built fires on the tree-less prairie with dried buffalo dung. It was their undoing. The white men knew that without buffalo the Indian could not survive.

When my playmate's grandfather No-Water was a teenager, the Sioux signed a peace treaty with General Sherman which agreed that they should forever have these Black Hills and the Dakota plains north of the Platte River. The ink was not yet dry when the white men began to trespass. In the next half-dozen years, over five million buffalo were slaughtered by whites as they built railroads through this Indian country. The days of the Sioux were numbered, since they fought with bow and arrow against the white man's cavalry. Finally they were subdued and herded onto the Pine Ridge Indian Reservation, which was located on the barren prairie a few miles east of Buffalo Gap. Some Indians fled the reservation traveling into Montana, where the famous battle of the Little Big Horn was fought at which General Custer and five companies of his command were wiped out. Chief Sitting Bull fled into Canada, where he endured ten bitterly cold winters. When at last his tribe returned to submit to life on the reservation, times were no better. It was a time of tumult: the ghost dance craze had worked the starving Sioux into a frenzy, Chief Sitting Bull was killed by Indian police under questionable circumstances, Chief Crazy Horse was assassinated by white soldiers, then during a blizzard at Christmas time the unthinkable happened. The Seventh Cavalry, who remained bitter over their defeat at the Little Big Horn, were watching the Indian encampment alongside the creek at Wounded Knee. Without provocation, the cavalry opened fire, much of it aimed at women and children. In this slaughter,

350 Sioux men, women, and children were murdered by the United States Cavalry in one of the more disgusting episodes in our nation's history. The winter was so cold that graves could not be dug in the frozen ground for days after the battle. A group of ranchers from Buffalo Gap rode their horses to the site and helped bury the dead, receiving $2.00 apiece for each grave.

SONG OF SITTING BULL

I-ki-di-ze   wa-on-kon
He   wa-na   he-na-la-ye-lo
He   i-yo-ti-ye   ki-ya-wa-on
A warrior
I have been.
Now
It is all over.
A hard time
I have.

On the July 4th celebrations in Buffalo Gap, we always had a rodeo and festivities. A dozen wagons of Sioux families would ride in from the reservation and pitch teepees in a vacant lot across from my father's bank, lured off the reservation by the prize money they could win as rodeo riders. The Indian women competed in horse-drawn wagon races down Main Street, also for prize money. This was our white man's celebration of a national holiday, but it was a religious celebration for the Sioux, who honored their Indian traditions in the shadow of Paha Sapa where they had feasted on buffalo in better days. After darkness fell, the Sioux met for a night of tribal dances around a camp fire. Several braves pounded on drums and chanted in a hypnotic, rhythmic beat, while other warriors in full tribal dress danced in a circle around the fire. The women in their long deer-hide robes stood off to one side and swayed in a heel dance to the beat of the drums. From the darkened shadows, we towns-people watched this spectacle that we knew was a passing pageant on the western scene.

The Sewright ranch across the road from us was a gathering place for Sioux Indians who came off the reservation during the summer to work. The rancher traded meat and other produce to the Indians who were destitute, and they moved to his ranch during the summer to work off their debts, living in tents alongside the creek. Their children became my playmates, and I learned their Sioux language. I was "Paha Sapa Ochela", a Black Hills boy. George No- Water was my age and a special friend. We rode stick horses around the neighborhood and through the ranch, and sometimes were permitted to ride real ponies. In a boyhood custom of that day, we made small cuts on our wrists and held them together in a symbolic exchange to become blood brothers. He became part white, and I became part Sioux. Perhaps it is this Sioux blood still coursing through my veins that gives me so much empathy for their cause.

Most of the white settlers arrived as cowboys trailing cattle herds from Texas on their way to Montana, who saw the empty land and staked their claim. Gene Griffis, who lived in the ranch house to the north of us, arrived trailing a herd of cattle and stayed. He was a tall, taciturn, quiet man of few words, a common trait for the old cowboys I knew. A beautiful lady, Anna, came from somewhere to marry and tame this cowboy. Even though she was a Christian, Gene never set foot inside a church, not that there was much of a church in town. Buffalo Gap was in need of law and order, so the sheriff came down from Custer and deputized Gene. Most the time he ranched, but when trouble was brewing he'd put on his badge, strap on his holster and head down town. He seldom had to draw his gun, because everyone in the territory knew he'd draw fast, shoot straight, and ask questions later. One year at the rodeo he shot Blutch Wilson, a rough neck halfbreed from the reservation. A drunken Blutch decided to ride his horse into the grandstand to say hello to some friends. The Deputy Sheriff ordered him to stop; an argument ensued, where-up-on Gene shot him. Gene Griffis was an old man who walked bent-over when I knew him. His pride was a son who was a Brigadier General in the U.S. Army, but in all the years I knew Gene his son never once came to Buffalo Gap for a visit with his father. I attended Gene's funeral when he died in his late eighties from the ravages of rheumatism. His son did not attend. How sad when priorities of life get screwed up.

In Buffalo Gap we lived the paradox of two cultures, one that admired the old Indian warriors, many of whom were our personal friends, yet another that treated them as third-class citizens-only a step away from a savage. This prejudice was underscored by federal law which forbade selling liquor to a Sioux. Our saloon had a sign on the door, "No Indians Allowed." All the white children could go into the saloon to buy candy, or we could stand at the bar and drink a coke, but no Indian could enter. These prejudices died with Buffalo Gap in the 1940's, when everyone moved away and left the town to the ghosts of the past.

Buffalo Gap had a diverse religious culture, all-be-it rather simple. Half the population - which never exceeded 186 souls during our time there - would have claimed some sort of religious culture even though few ever attended services. The first church services were Episcopalian, which were held in the stage coach station by a missionary bishop who occasionally passed though town. It was not until 50 years later that an Episcopal church was built, and even then its services were held sporadically by traveling missionaries. While the Episcopalians were holding occasional services in homes, it was not the same as having a church building in town. One evening as a group of cowboys were gathered in the saloon drinking and playing poker, they all agreed that Buffalo Gap needed a church, so a jar was placed at the end of the bar. The jar was left there for some months until there was enough to begin construction of a church. A carpenter who was also an ordained Congregationalist minister was hired to build the church and conduct services. So the town had a church, but fifteen years later the membership and money had declined, so the church was sold to the Baptists, who had an infusion of money from religious philanthropists in the East. Again membership declined, and the church was closed. The bell in the steeple, the pulpit, and all the pews were sold. Five years later a fund raising campaign under the auspices of the city fathers was successful; the church property was purchased from the Baptists and established as a Methodist church. But it had no bell, pulpit or pews. So Julius Gerber, who ran the saloon, donated the money to purchase these from an abandoned church up in Sturgis. Buffalo Gap again had a church and hired a minister, who had to supplement his income with other work. It was at this time that the Keating family moved to Buffalo Gap from Camp Crook, and we kids attended the Methodist Sunday School on the Sundays when a Catholic missionary did not make it to town.

A Catholic church had been built by the diocese, but at no time was a priest ever assigned, and it was serviced by traveling missionaries on a part-time basis. We were one of only five families that attended when the missionary priest came every third or fourth week. During the bitter cold of winter it was uncertain if he could make it through the snow drifts, so we awaited his arrival in our warm homes. If he made it, he'd drive through town honking his horn, and then we'd all rush down to the church.

In those pre-Vatican Two days, the priest had to fast from all food and water until after his last Communion of the day, so by the time he got to Buffalo Gap he was reeling from hunger and thirst. One of the duties of an altar boy was to leave in mid-service, going next door to Mel's Service Station to get a cup of coffee, carry it back and place it on the left corner of the altar. After the priest finished the Last Gospel and genuflected, he took a big gulp of coffee, and then turned to face the congregation and administer the final blessing.

In those days the priest always said the Mass in Latin, facing the altar with his back to the parish, and no one except himself understood any Latin or knew much about the liturgy. We all stood, kneeled, stood again, and sat on cue. Grandma Hackle may have prayed, and if so, she was probably the only one who did much of it. My mother spent her time keeping us five kids in the front pew quiet. Dad sat looking bored. Mostly, I just waited for it to be over. If I ever had a genuine religious experience in that church, I don't recall when it was.

My mother had been raised a Methodist. On the Sundays when the missionary did not hold services, our mother would take us to Sunday school in the Methodist Church. We learned about the Golden Rule, the King James Bible, and sang the hymn *Onward Christians Soldiers*. There was no confusion in mixing the two religions as a child, because they existed in two separate worlds, neither of them the real one in which we lived. Religion was something you did on Sundays, but other times you did things because they were right or wrong - you didn't need a Bible or Catechism for that.

So our religion in Buffalo Gap was hewn to the rough and tumble of a small, isolated community. No matter. Religion was not a big issue in anyone's lives, and Sunday services were only a traditional pageant to adorn the weekend. People were struggling enough during those depression years just to keep a roof overhead and food on the table; needless controversy among religious faiths was a burden no one needed.

If I could relive my youth, I would spend more time searching the religious roots of the Sioux. I would ask No-Water's grandfather about life on the prairie in a teepee. What was it like to camp here at Buffalo Gap with the Sioux tribes and join in the hunt? What about the spirits, his Gods, and the vision of the White Buffalo? I would love to visit again with Chief High Eagle; perhaps he would share with me again the events of that day at the Little Big Horn. I would spend time with Black Elk and talk about his anguish at Wounded Knee. Here is something this old Sioux warrior wrote many years later.

Black Elk's Lament

"I did not know then how much was ended.
When I look back now from this high hill
of my old age, I can still see the butchered
women and children lying heaped and scattered

all along the crooked gulch as plain
as when I saw them with eyes still young.
And I can see that something else died
there in the bloody mud, and was buried in
the blizzard. A people's dream died there.

It was a beautiful dream . . .
The nation's hoop is broken and scattered.
There is no center any longer,
and the sacred tree is dead."

BLACK ELK

8
THE CHRISTIAN FAITH

Religion: "Concern over what exists beyond the visible world, differentiated from philosophy in that it operates through faith or intuition rather than reason, and generally includes the idea of the existence of a single being (or other spiritual entity) that has created the world and governs it, as well as the idea that prayer, rituals, or certain principles of everyday conduct are spiritually rewarding."

Some people refer to their "religious philosophy". This combination of contradictory words is an oxymoron. Philosophy is based on reason; religion is not, and operates through faith or intuition rather than reason. I have listened to arguments where the proponents attempted to prove their religion was the correct one by using the process of reason. That is a fruitless effort; if one has a religion; it is found only on the basis of faith or intuition.

I've spent a lifetime riding the fence lines of my Christian faith in which the boundaries were defined by my upbringing with the Catholic catechism and Methodist Sunday school. Since I have relied on much of my knowledge of Judaism, Islam, and Buddhism on secular history books and the encyclopedia, I decided that in pursuit of a level playing field I should return to these same secular literature sources for a look at my Christian faith. So I will attempt to set aside my prejudices, telling the story of Christianity as it is related by historians and the encyclopedia, the same references I utilized for my look at other religious faiths. That is a different approach than normal, because most Christians look at their faith only from the perspective of how it is related in the Bible. I'm sure this secular account will upset some Christians.

One must begin a look at the Christian faith with the New Testament. If there were no New Testament there would likely be no Christian religion, because other historical accounts for the existence of Jesus are rather meager. Pliny the Younger, who was the foremost Roman historian of that era, makes no reference to the existence of Christ in the Roman Territory. "The Roman historian, Tacitus, is among the earliest allusions to him outside the New Testament." The principle Jewish historian of the era, Flavius Josephus, refers to John the Baptist, but as a result of various translations it is debatable if he records anything concerning the ministry of Jesus. "Josephus's importance to the Christian world derives from a Slavonic edition of his works, in which he writes of Jesus, 'and there arose a man, if you could indeed call him a man'. If this passage was truly written by Josephus, it would be the only relatively contemporaneous passage outside the New Testament (aside from Tacitus's) notation of Jesus crucifixion that speaks of Jesus. But virtually all scholars today believe that the paragraph about Jesus was inserted later by a Christian writer, and is definitely a forgery". There exist pseudepigrapha articles (certain writings professing to be Biblical in character, but not considered canonical or inspired) that allegedly make reference to Jesus, but their authorship is suspect. Almost our only resources of information about the personality of Jesus are derived from the four Gospels, and from allusions to his life in the letters (epistles) of the early Christian propagandists. Many historians believe the first three Gospels of Matthew, Mark, and Luke were derived from some earlier documents; the Gospel of St. John came later and was published in AD 90, sixty years after the death of Jesus. Jesus is also mentioned in the Islamic Koran, but this document originated five centuries after his death.

Because Jesus himself left not a single written word behind, and because contemporary non-Christian historians did not mention him, some historians in recent centuries denied the historicity of Jesus. Perhaps the strongest support for his existence outside the four Gospels is found in the Jewish Talmud which made allusions to miracles attributed to Jesus, although his name is not mentioned therein. Modern scholarship is widely agreed that in the past two centuries the historical method has frequently been applied to the Biblical records in a biased way. The Gospel writers place their material in a supernatural framework, and miracles are an essential part of their records. When the supernatural features are stripped from the Gospels, a "historical Jesus" is difficult to discover.

Sacred books are found in a number of other religions, but the Bible is unique in several respects. Divine authority is claimed for it. The Bible is not just a record of a divine revelation, as the Koran and the sacred books of Buddhism also claim to be; rather, the making of the Bible is itself part of the divine history which it reveals.

I was taught this bedtime prayer in Sunday school.

> **Matthew, Mark,**
> **Luke, and John,**
> **Bless this bed**
> **That I lay on.**

These four guys, Matthew, Mark, Luke, and John wrote the four Gospels, all in the Greek language. These Gospels, which stand first among the twenty-seven books of the New Testament, record the birth, ministry of teaching and miracles, death, and resurrection of Jesus Christ. The dates and authorship of the Gospels has been the subject of much research and debate. Since they do not refer by name to their authors, and since the titles were added not earlier than a generation or two after their composition, one must rely on meager internal evidence and patristic traditions that date from the second and succeeding centuries. Many modern scholars believe that the Gospels of Matthew and Luke were written after, and based on the Gospel of Mark. Mark was the companion and assistant of Paul (and afterwards with Peter), who wrote down the remembrances of Peter concerning the ministry of Christ. This was done about A.D. 65, three decades after the death of Christ. Critics are disposed to regard the Gospel of St. Mark as being the earliest and the most trustworthy account of the personality and actual words of Jesus.

The authorship of the Gospel of John is also debated, it having more idiosyncrasies and colored by theology of a strongly Hellenic type. Many Christians believe it was written by the Apostle John at Ephesus during the last decade of the first century. Most modern scholars believe that the Apostle John was not the author, but that his testimony underlies the work of other Evangelists who may have been his disciples.

Let us now look at the beginnings of the Christian religion as it is contained in the Bible. We know virtually nothing about Jesus from his time as a small child until he came to John the Baptist along the Sea of Galilee at about the age of thirty. He is believed to have spent his life in Nazareth, a hill town of Galilee, the northern part of Palestine. By inference from the Gospels, we believe he was a carpenter or mason. He was brought up in the atmosphere of a pious Jewish home, in the synagogue he learned to read, and was educated. His public career was ushered in by his baptism through John the Baptist. John, a prophetic personality of great power, proclaimed that God was to bring about a decisive change in the history of mankind. When Jesus was baptized, a divine voice confirmed that he was the promised Messiah of the coming Kingdom of God. The early part of his ministry was in Judea, closely related to John the Baptist's work. When the latter was arrested by King Herod Antipas, Jesus shifted the center of his activity to Galilee.

Jesus' ministry consisted in proclaiming God's kingdom, or kingship; that is, that God himself was about to assume directly the government of this world. This message was preached to the crowds which soon flocked to him, both in the synagogues and in large open-air meetings. People were deeply impressed by his grandeur and power, awed by his moral supremacy and his mysteriousness, frightened and kept in deep reverence by his closeness to God, and yet personally attracted to him by his kindness and humility. With all this, however, he remained enigmatic even to his most intimate followers during his lifetime. No one could keep neutral in his presence. While an increasing number regarded him as a divine messenger, other circles grew in their antagonism.

Jesus gathered around himself twelve followers who he trained for the task of proclaiming his message. The decisive event in his public career took place when Simon Peter, one of the twelve, confessed that he believed that Jesus was the promised Messiah, though Jesus had never made such a claim in the presence of his disciples. At that moment Jesus told his disciples that he considered Peter's confession as the voice of God, and said that the disciples were destined to be the nucleus of his chosen people, who would continue his work in history. This was the charter of the Christian church.

Being aware of the contrast between his claims and interpretation of God's will with that held by the official representatives of the Jewish religion, Jesus decided in AD 30 to go to Jerusalem for the first time and challenge his adversaries. He did this the week before the Passover when hundreds of thousands of pilgrims thronged in the city. He was well received by many people, however, the representatives of the official religion did not take kindly to this critic in their midst. On Thursday night he assembled his disciples secretly for a solemn meal, the last supper. There he broke bread and wine in a ritual that was to become central to the Christian Mass. At this supper, Jesus explained the mystery of his mission. As bread has to be broken to be eaten, and wine has to be consumed if it is to be enjoyed, so he interpreted his life as an act of self-giving and indicated that out of his death new life would grow.

One of his disciples betrayed to authorities the place on the slopes of the Mount of Olives to which Jesus and his disciples withdrew during the nights. He was arrested; quickly tried before the Sanhedrin, the supreme court of the Jews; convicted of blasphemy upon his statement that he was the Messiah and the Son of God; and sentenced to death. He was handed over to the Roman official, the Procurator Pontius Pilot, the charge being that rebellion was implied in his confession that he was the Messianic ruler. The Procurator doubted his guilt, but put the problem to the people in his audience and received their verdict of death for Jesus.

He was crucified on a knoll outside the gates of the city, and was buried the same evening. But followers of his who came to the tomb on Sunday found the tomb empty. Jesus appeared to various groups of his followers during the first weeks after his death; he was seen in bodily form, but could not be contained by walls and closed doors; and he disappeared as suddenly as he had appeared. A number of hypotheses have been offered to explain away the miracle of the resurrection of Jesus, but they all do violence to the records.

According to some scholars, there was nothing new and original in the message of Jesus. For each of his sayings, parallels have been pointed out in the Old Testament or in rabbinical literature. Others, on the contrary, claim that the teaching of Jesus was completely unique and unexampled. Against the latter view, there are Jesus' own words that he came to fulfill the Old Testament, not to destroy it, and thus that all he taught was in continuity and harmony with it.

Two contentions in his teachings were unique: the time of his ministry was the turning point in history, when God started to transform the world; and he was appointed to usher in this new age. Because of this, the ideas of God, man, time, and the world all appeared in an entirely new guise.

At one point during his ministry, a disciple came to him and asked that he teach them to pray. Jesus responded, "In this manner therefore shall you pray":

THE LORD'S PRAYER

Our Father who art in heaven,
Hallowed be thy name.
Thy kingdom come,
Thy will be done
On earth, as it is in heaven.

Give us this day our daily
Bread.
And forgive us our debts, as
We also forgive our debtors.
And lead us not into temptation,
But deliver us from evil.

This simple prayer addressed the philosophies of his Father in Heaven, the

Kingdom of God, and the relationship of man to each other.

Jesus considered his life and death both as atonement for the sins of mankind, and as a source of the new supernatural power of the spirit to be given to those who believed in his mission. Within weeks after his death, his followers who had stayed behind in Jerusalem succeeded in winning large numbers of persons to believe that Jesus was the promised Messiah. The movement grew and spread over the Mediterranean world and Near East.

Presently there arose a second great teacher, whom many modern authorities regard as the real founder of Christianity - Saul of Tarsus, or Paul. By birth he was probably a Jew, and had studied under Jewish teachers, but he was well versed in the Hellenic theologies of Alexandra, and his language was Greek. Paul had never seen Jesus. He was not one of the twelve disciples, but became a later convert. Three years after his conversion in Jerusalem, he met St. Peter and St. James, and began to preach. In AD 44, a decade after the death of Jesus, Paul began extensive journeys throughout the Mediterranean world that were to continue through his life, and he was martyred in Rome about AD 68. When I visited the Forum in Rome, I saw the cave-type jail where St. Paul is thought to have been confined.

It was as early as with Paul that the teachings of Jesus began to take on new meanings. He was the first of many later Christian leaders, such as Augustine, who began to embellish the simple religion of Jesus with complexities. What Jesus preached was a new birth of the human soul; what Paul preached, additionally, was the ancient religion of priests and altar and the propitiatory bloodshed. Jesus was to him the Easter lamb, that traditional human victim who haunted the preceding religions of that region, particularly that of Mithraism, a cult of the Near East. These teachings of Paul provided the Nazarenes and other early Christians with a satisfactory explanation of the disaster of the crucifixion, an event that had been utterly perplexing to them. This gave them a spirit of hope, and Paul left them as Christians with the beginning of a creed.

Simon Peter, a native of Galilee and a fisherman, was chosen by Jesus to be one of the twelve apostles. At the time of Peter's confession of faith,

Christ made statements that remain controversial to this day. Roman Catholics interpret these words as a promise of primacy of jurisdiction which is to abide in the Church of Christ to the end of time, which postulates successors of Peter in the same office. Others interpret the words as a promise to all the apostles through Peter, or at the most, as a personal prerogative of Peter, which died with him.

Very little of Peter's later life is known. He died a martyr in Rome sometime during the years AD 64-67. There is a tradition, dating from the end of the second century, that he exercised the office of the Bishop of Rome. St. Linus is listed by the Liberian catalogue as the second Pope but little is known about him. The history of the papacy is confusing because of the multitude and abundance of the popes. They mostly began to reign as old men, and their reigns were short, averaging less than two years each.

Much of the history of the Christians in the first two centuries is very obscure. They spread far and wide throughout the world, but we know very little of their ideas or their ceremonies and methods during that time. As yet they had no settled creeds and there can be little doubt that there were wide local variations in their beliefs and disciplines during this formless period.

Early Christians in Rome were persecuted and remained underground for a couple centuries until the time of the Roman leader Constantine, who became a Christian. In AD 325, a watershed event of Christianity occurred at Nicea where the first general (ecumenical) council of the Christian world was held. At this ecumenical council, the Nicene Creed was written and it established the definition of Christian teaching. This creed was endorsed by all Christians long before the split with the Eastern Orthodox or the Protestants which came many centuries later. It has been revised over the centuries, but still remains a part of the Roman Catholic Mass, and a litmus test of belief for those who would be a Roman Catholic.

NICENE CREED

Credo in unum deum
Patrem omnipotentem.
Factorem caeli et terra
Visibiliuim omnium,
et in visibilium..............

Perhaps the English translation is better understood, so let's start over with the version as it was said at the Catholic Mass during my youth prior to the Vatican Two council.

I believe in one God, The Father Almighty,
maker of heaven and earth, and of all things
visible and invisible. And in one Lord Jesus Christ,
the only-begotten Son of God. Born of the Father
before all ages. God of God, light of light,
true God of true God. Begotten not made;
being of one substance with the Father;
by whom all things were made. Who for us men,
and for our salvation, came down from heaven.
AND WAS INCARNATE BY THE HOLY GHOST
OF THE VIRGIN MARY: AND WAS MADE MAN.
He was crucified also for us, suffered under
Pontius Pilate, and was buried. And the third day
He rose again according to the Scriptures.
And ascended into heaven. He sitteth at the
right hand of the Father. And He shall
come again with glory to judge both the living
and the dead; of whose kingdom there shall be no end.
And I believe in the Holy Ghost, the Lord
and giver of life: Who proceedeth from the
Father and the Son. Who together
with the Father and the Son is adored and glorified.
Who spake by the Prophets. And in one, holy,
catholic and apostolic Church. I confess
one baptism for the remission of sins.
And I look for the resurrection of the dead.
And the life of the world to come. Amen.

The impact that Paul had on the early thinking of the church is underscored by Pope John Paul ll. in his book *Crossing the Threshold of Hope*, "The words of the Nicene Creed are nothing other than the reflection of Paul's doctrine." The Pope then discusses the direction the church theology took in this era:

> **"Then, beginning in the fourth century the Nicene-Constantinopolitan Creed entered into catechetical and liturgical use, enriching her teaching. It enriched that teaching thanks to the increased awareness which the Church gained as she progressively entered into Greek culture and more clearly realized the need for ways of presenting her doctrine which would be adequate and convincing in that cultural context."**

By the fourth century of the Era, we find all the Christian communities so agitated and exasperated by tortuous and elusive arguments about the nature of God as to be largely negligent of the simpler teachings of charity, service, and brotherhood that Jesus had inculcated.

The history of the Christian religion from its inception through the middle ages, the reformation, and on to modern times is one of turmoil, conflict, and struggle. Long before our time, the Popes were riding a lot of fence lines. As a cowboy riding fences on the infidel prairies of Dakota, how much about the early Christian church was I expected to know before I discovered a Christian religious philosophy? And would the history even lead me there, because all religions are based on faith and intuition, not on reason. That's why they are called a "faith". That is heavy lifting for a cowboy.

9

I'M A TIPPERARY MAN

By Father Michael Kelly
Pastor, Catholic Church

I'm a Tipperary man. That's true in spite of the fact that I was born in Dublin. That's true in spite of the fact that I have spent more than half my life six thousand miles away from Tipperary. That's true in spite of the fact that only one of my five siblings now lives in our native county. Ask someone from the United States where they are from and the first word out of their mouth will be the city or the state, but never the county. Ask anyone from Ireland where they are from, and the first thing you will hear is the name of the county. The two most popular sports in Ireland are Gaelic football and hurling; they are played by amateurs, i.e. non-paid athletes, and the biggest rivalry is county versus county. Each year, in both sports, we have All-Ireland finals, where each county vies to be champion. Large numbers travel all over the country to support their county, and to be champion of all of Ireland is a coveted title indeed.

Tipperary is in the Republic of Ireland, which is more than 90% Catholic, and the distinctive unit, especially in rural Ireland, is the parish. Place names in Ireland are now commonly referred to in the English language, but come from the original Gaelic or Irish language name of the place. I grew up in the village and parish of Ballingarry, from the original Gaelic

Baile an Garrai, literally the town of the garden. Now why it was ever called that I don't know, because I never saw a garden in our little area. Our parish bordered on County Kilkenny, and Tipperary was a fierce rival of Kilkenny in hurling. Nobody felt that rivalry more that those who lived right beside county borders, and, to complicate matters, our parents were both from County Kilkenny. So were all my uncles and aunts and some of my cousins. Whenever we played against Kilkenny, it would be both an exhilarating time and a time for fear; the joy of beating them was almost as extreme as the sadness if we met defeat. This would have been even truer in the days before other distractions, like television, came along, in rural Ireland's case, in 1962.

In view of all this, it was a brave venture for my parents to move from their native Kilkenny to this little village in Tipperary in 1947 and buy a small house with a view to opening a little store. They begun by selling pots of jelly through one of the windows and, by means of very hard work and dedicated and personal service, built the store into a successful business, which enabled them to raise and educate their six children.

For 800 years, various British governments have tried to subjugate the Irish people and rule them from London. The Irish can hardly be blamed, therefore, for staying neutral in the Second World War. When Germany invaded Poland in 1939, it was a bare 17 years since the Irish had gotten their freedom after those eight centuries of oppression. However, quite a number of Irishmen did what my Father did, and went to Britain to join the fight against Hitler. He ended up in the R.A.F., the Royal Air Force and was in a ground crew for the duration of the war. He was engaged to my Mother in 1939 but, because of the war, they couldn't be married until 1945.

My Mother came from a family that had a very small store and she worked in that store from an early age. She obviously learned well and quickly, because all of her life she was well known as a very astute businesswoman. For most of their business lives, our parents worked long and hard hours, usually taking only a half-day off on Sundays. Most people inherit a lot of their personal traits from their parents and I often think that my own reluctance to take a regular day off or even an evening off comes from the example I got from my parents.

As contradictory as it seems, I have never felt, either then or now, that our parents working so hard took from their time for or dedication to us. Perhaps because the store and house were the same building - very much the norm in Ireland - we were in close proximity all day every day. Being the oldest of the children, I helped out in the store from a very early age. A number of older people have told me they would come in every morning when I was 5 years old and have me read the headlines in the paper to them. On reflection, serving the customers of the store for many years was a good preparation for my eventually serving people in various parishes, since it made it easier to meet people and deal with their needs.

I haven't made a study of climatic conditions in Ireland in the 1950s, but many people of my age seem to think that the summers were sunnier and warmer then and the periods around Christmas had more snow. Whether that is actually true or whether it's selective memory as we grow older, I don't know. But many of my most vivid memories of childhood are of wonderful sunny days playing soccer in our backyard or in the field next door; of going through field after field until we found almost-secret swimming places and of my childhood best friend and I and our brothers, two years younger, almost having the courage to stay overnight in a makeshift tent when we were 10 years old beside one of these rivers. Hunger and the dark changed our minds. In an overgrown weed and reed field opposite our store, we spent many happy hours playing cowboys and Indians. Our only knowledge of what cowboys and Indians meant would have come from twice a year movies in a local hall, and from comic books. This was still the pre-television era in rural Ireland and we had to make up our own amusements and games, so our imaginations and creative juices were constantly being exercised. On reflection, so many of today's pastimes are things that people have done for them, so I'm grateful that our generation had to conjure theses games and activities for ourselves.

Religion was a big part of our lives at that time, although we would never have though of it as such, because it was automatic. Every Sunday and holy day we would go to church, which in my case was literally next-door. Many of my friends said to me in those young days: "I don't know how you live beside a graveyard; it must be very scary". However, the only time I can ever remember being afraid was late one night when coming home from a scary movie about vampires at the local hall. My brother and I ran like crazy past the broad church entrance, which contained many headstones that seemed to glow in the reflected moonlight on this particular night.

When I think back on the spirituality of my parents, it's obvious that each had quite an effect on me. My Mother was the more obviously spiritual one, the one who led us in our family prayers every night and who made sure we received the sacraments regularly. My Dad was less obviously religious, but he was a very honest, hard-working man who would never miss Mass and was great for going to funerals and showing others, by doing that, that they counted and mattered. Some people in Ireland went to funerals because there was always the pub afterwards, but my Dad didn't drink, so that was of no interest to him. My Mother would always be praying for somebody or some special intention of others, and again, it is only now that I recognize the wonderful example she gave to me of being concerned for other people.

I was born in 1949. I became an altar server at the age of 7, when I received my First Communion. That meant learning Latin or, more accurately, memorizing the Latin responses in the Mass. A man who had a big impact on my life, though I didn't realize it at the time, was the local curate, or associate pastor, who was a friend of the family. He often dropped in to the house and owned a truly revolutionary item for this time in rural Ireland: a film projector. From time to time on a Sunday night, after the store was closed, he would show the whole family films that would enthrall us. Looking back on them now, I realize that most were educational short films, but to us who had never experienced TV, seeing those flickering images on a sheet at the end of the store was like seeing magic tricks right in front of our eyes. He was a priest who knew the people of his parish and who took wonderful care of them. He was also the one who oversaw the renovation of the church building when Vatican II told us to return to our roots and turn the altar around to face the people and have Mass in our own language. He wasn't young when these big changes occurred, but he implemented them with an enthusiasm that I admire with every passing year.

This priest also had an influence on me in that he was interested in literature and art and maintained that there was more theology in a good novel than in most theology books. Long before Vatican II, I remember him saying that there was such a waste in the church, particularly of nuns who had talents in this area or that but that were slotted, with no choice of their own, into teaching where frustrations, understandably, showed themselves in various ways. I came to learn from him to be continuously open to God speaking to us through many things of "the world" in addition to what would be generally regarded as things that pertained to God.

In my 50 years of living, in my 27 years as a priest, that is one observation I would happily say I have learned, or to be more accurate, am learning more and more each day: that God is not in a box, let alone a box defined by human beings of whatever faith. God is, as we learned in school at the age of 5, "everywhere" and wars and strife and hatreds and hostilities and tortures and maiming and death have resulted in people trying to force one group of people into their definition of God, the God they see in their box. It is impossible in human terms to define God, but the patience God has shown to us human beings who are far too often so intolerant of others prompts me to believe that one of the defining characteristics of God is tolerance. If we are to be imitators of the God we worship and adore, tolerance is our first step toward that Supreme Being.

In the 60s, high school in Ireland meant 5 years, 8th through 12th grade. One of the major dates on the calendar of Irish history is 1966 when the Government official in charge of education introduced "free education". Ireland and its economic revival owe a lot to this concept i.e. everyone was entitled to a high school education, regardless of income. However, since I started high school in 1962, the only way I could go to high school was to boarding school. At the time, that meant that, at the age of 13, for 5 years in a row, I left home on September 1st and got a two-week break for Christmas and a two-week break for Easter. Apart from that, boarding school students were away from home from the beginning of September until the middle of June. I have heard many people complain bitterly about boarding schools of our era but I would have to say that, with the exception of a couple of teachers who wielded a cane on our hands like there was no tomorrow, my memories are mostly good. Why these particular teachers thought the world was going to end if we didn't know the second person plural of the pluperfect of some obscure Latin or Greek verb escapes me, but nowadays I put it down to the theory that these people must have been trapped in their own, tiny version of what the world should be.

A Funny Thing Happened On The Way To London
(I became a priest)

I have been asked by many of my parishioners when I decided to become a priest. A neighbor in the village informed me, when I visited her home on the day I was ordained, that I had told her, at the age of 5, that I was going to be a priest someday. I don't remember that. I do recall that, during my first year of high school, I had a list of occupations I was thinking of, perhaps a somewhat typical list for a 13 year old of that era: astronaut, jet pilot, professional soccer player, journalist, train driver or priest. I don't know how I would have done at the other careers of choice, but the deciding factor about what to do with my life came in the summer before my senior year in high school.

I decided to work in a factory in England to earn money for College. During that summer, I came across many people who had a lot of material things, a lot of comforts that money could buy, but who seemed to have a great emptiness in their lives. Virtually none of them had any faith in God nor did they see any need for spirituality, or at least that's what they told me. It gradually dawned on me during that summer that one way to fill that emptiness in the lives of people like my co-workers would be to help bring Christianity to them by becoming a priest. During my senior year in high school I decided to enter the seminary in the fall.

The first decision you have to make, after you decide to be a priest, is what kind of priest you wanted to be. One option would be to join a Religious Order, and there were many of those. However, most religious order priests that I knew about at that age were involved in teaching and I knew I didn't want to spend my life as a priest as a teacher in a classroom. Another option was to go on what was called the "foreign missions", mostly to nations in Asia and Africa. This had quite a draw for me, but I decided not to do it because, whatever academic gifts I had, foreign languages were very definitely not my strength. It was very tempting to become a priest and serve in Ireland, since I came from a close family and would have loved to stay in close proximity to them. But I felt very strongly that, if I was going to become a priest, I wanted to serve in a place where priests were definitely needed.

I finished high school in June 1967 and entered the seminary in September of that year. This seminary was for those studying mainly for the English-speaking "missions", which in my time meant mainly the United States and Britain. From the time you enter, it's 6 years to ordination as a priest. During the first year, each student had to decide which diocese to spend the rest of his life serving in. We had access to various kinds of statistics about those dioceses that were looking for priests. In addition, priests from some of these dioceses would come and speak to the uncommitted students. I chose the diocese of Stockton, California, partly because it was a relatively small diocese and partly because it had been created from parts of San Francisco and Sacramento dioceses in 1962 and had been left short of priests. Apart from those two facts, I knew nothing of this place I was committing to for the rest of my life.

Looking back on it now, it seems it looks like a foolhardy thing to have done at the age of 18, to decide to go to a place six thousand miles from Ireland to an area where I knew nobody to do something I was a long way from being trained to do. But at that time, Ireland was still a country that was very high in the percentage of Catholic practice of the faith and part of that faith, handed down to us in our history classes as well as our religious classes in grade school and high school, was the concept of spreading Christianity throughout the world. The 60s were a time of great change all over the western world, although perhaps less so in Ireland than in other countries, but with the advent of better economic times and education available to everyone, there was a visible change in seminaries throughout the land.

In the seminary where I studied, and there were 5 others just like ours in Ireland, training for English-speaking missions, the change can be seen dramatically in the 6 years I was there. 29 of us started in 1967. On average, 50% of the beginning number would end up being ordained six years later. The year after we started, 30 entered. But in September 1970, only 18 came in and that drop was reflected all over Ireland. What we didn't know then, as we begun this new decade, was that 18 were going to look high in comparison to future classes. The numbers continued to drop through the 80s and have only made a token recovery in the late 90s. This is true throughout the western church, although the seminaries in parts of the third world are doing much better. It will be ironic when Asia and Africa, where so many missionaries went to in order to spread the gospel of Christ, will produce the bulk of priests to serve the western world. Actually, it's already beginning to happen.

The seminary ended up being a good experience for me. The 6-year course included a major in theology and a minor in philosophy and we studied a lot of scripture in addition to dogmatic and moral theology. Our class started the seminary at a time when the reforms of the Second Vatican Council, Vatican II, were being implemented and so we were blessed to have some enlightened professors who helped us to see the mystery of God far beyond the somewhat narrow learned-by-heart definitions most of us grew up with. One of the many wonderful results of Vatican II was the decentralization of power and decision-making in the church, a trend that, sadly, has been largely reversed in the past twenty years. Because of this opening-up of attitudes to so many aspects of God and the way we can experience God's actions in our lives, I believe that, in general, the priests ordained in the 1970s are more open to change and to the ideas of other faiths than those ordained either before or after that decade.

Since I mentioned people of other faiths, this may be a good time to talk about the problems in Northern Ireland. Since 1969, there has been fighting in the six counties that make up the political entity, called Northern Ireland, which was created by the British government in 1921. In those counties, the proportion of Protestant to Catholic is approximately 60% to 40%. It always irks me that most Americans are presented with the difficulties in Northern Ireland as a purely religious struggle. In actual fact, the conflict is a complicated socio-economic struggle with a lot of history behind it, but that doesn't make as newsworthy a headline as Protestant versus Catholic. Three hundred and fifty years ago the British government, who militarily controlled Ireland at the time, transplanted a large number people from Scotland to Ireland, mostly around the northeast counties of the island. These planters were given the land and the Irish were thrown off their land, essentially becoming slaves on their own land. Because the transplantation happened after the Reformation, those brought over from Scotland happened to be Protestant and those who were evicted from their homes and property were Catholic.

If you think of the great variety of countries and religions and philosophies that made up the immigrants to the United States in the 19th century and the early part of the 20th century, it's amazing that they all blended and got along as well as they did. I would strongly maintain that the great breaker-down of barriers is intermarriage. When someone from one background marries someone from a different background, whatever prejudices they both bring begin to be broken down by that marriage. In turn, when their children, in turn, marry, the barriers are broken down even more. That breaking down of barriers never happened in Northern Ireland because intermarriage never happened, but it's important to understand why. They didn't marry, not because one was Protestant and the other was Catholic but because one was master and the other was slave. Master doesn't marry slave, and therefore what might well have brought the communities together, intermarriage, was forbidden by the caste system.

Therefore, it is important to realize that those who are Protestants in Northern Ireland are the direct descendants of the people who were given the land nearly four centuries ago. Those who are Catholics are the direct descendants of those who were thrown off their land. So, when the term

Protestant and Catholic are used in the context of Northern Ireland, they are actually ethnic terms much more than religious terms.

In 1968, no doubt inspired by the successes of the Rev. Martin Luther King Jr. and his campaign for human rights, people began marching in Northern Ireland for many of the same kinds of rights. Many Catholics in the area didn't have a vote and many were unable to own their own property. As fundamental as these two rights are, the basic problem and one of the ongoing difficulties has been the right to a job. In many places of employment in Northern Ireland, there were signs up saying "Catholics need not apply". Over and over again, a Protestant would be given a job ahead of a much more qualified Catholic. Particularly since 1922, most factories and other places of employment built in Northern Ireland were built in the heavily Protestant area, leading to horrendous unemployment in the Catholic areas.

I visited the city of Derry (renamed Londonderry by the British, but never called that by any Catholic) during the cease-fire of 1971 and met a man there who was about 50 years old. He was Catholic and had two sons, aged 24 and 18. He told me that his Grandfather before him never had a job or a chance of a job; neither had his Father; neither had he. He said "Maybe that was good enough for my Grandfather, maybe that was good enough for my Father, maybe even that's good enough for me, since, like them, I am powerless to do anything about it. But I can't stand by and pass that same kind of heritage onto my sons." It was people like him and his sons who begun marching in 1968 and fighting in 1969. Please understand that I wouldn't begin to justify the horrendous violence that this part of Ireland has suffered; so many innocent people have died, so many have been injured, so much property has been damaged. But if you know some of the historical background to the situation, you can see that people like this man and his sons felt like something had to be done, or there would never be equal opportunity for the minority.

By the early 1970s, the British government had stepped in and imposed direct rule from London; Catholics now had a vote, though the gerrymandering of the districts ensured that their representation would not be in proportion to the population. But when the government tried to force equal job opportunity on those in power, a general strike was called and the British in London backed down. It was a wonderful opportunity let go by a government that lost its nerve - and its principals.

As I write this, things are at a delicate impasse. On the one hand those who want to continue union with Britain are asked to share the power they have held onto with an ironclad fist for so long. On the other hand, the Irish Republican Army had refused to relinquish any of their arms, showing the same kind of unyielding inflexibility that has condemned the area to such non-ending conflict. Recently, they agreed to these weapons being inspected by independent inspectors, which bring new optimism for the future. Caught in the middle are the vast majority of Protestants and Catholics, who would like to see peace and stability in their area. I have given a talk about the historical background to the conflict in Northern Ireland to many service groups and church social gatherings of various denominations in the last 27 years in California, and I always leave time for questions afterwards. Invariably I am asked "when will they ever stop fighting?" The answer I give is amazingly simple and amazingly complex. It's one of the mottoes of Pope Paul VI: "If you want peace, work for justice". Until there is true justice for all the people of Northern Ireland, there won't be true peace.

August 25th 1973 is a date that will always remain in my memory. It was the day I left Ireland to begin my work as a priest in California. I was ordained two months earlier at the age of 23, I turned 24 in July and now I was at Shannon airport with my family, taking a step that many Irish priests and religious had taken in the past, leaving our native shores to further the Gospel of Christ in a distant land. One big difference from those who had left decades earlier is that I knew I would be back for vacation in a year, but that didn't make leaving any easier. The Aer Lingus flight was delayed, and I didn't want to have my family hanging around for hours, not knowing when we would depart, so I told them to go. Walking down that wooden corridor with my bags on a trolley, I felt a surge of aloneness that I had never felt before.

That dissipated somewhat when I got on board the 747, still a new kind of plane at the time and to me it was so huge and amazing. Remember that, at the age of 13, being a pilot was one of my dreams, so it was fascinating to me how this city on wheels could actually get off the ground. We landed at Logan airport in Boston just days after the first reported plane crash officially attributed to wind shear. Then on to San Francisco. Since that day, I have flown many, many times into SFO, and never since then did the pilot announce that he was flying over Stockton. But that day the pilot said, "If you look out the right side of the plane you will see the city of Stockton." Since I had committed myself for the rest of my life to the people of the diocese of Stockton, I looked down and there it was, baking in the summer sun. That was my second strong feeling of aloneness, and I asked myself, what I am doing here, so many miles from home, coming to an area where I know no one at all.

Actually, I had only one more feeling along those lines, on my first weekend at my first parish in Modesto. The pastor, another Tipperary man, said to me "We usually greet people at the doors after Mass", a practice foreign to me, having never seen it done anywhere in Ireland. I didn't say it to the pastor, but I did say to myself, how can I do that, since I don't know any of these people. Which is really ironic, since, for most of my priesthood I have made it a practice to greet parishioners not just after Mass, but before every Mass, whether I am celebrating the Mass or not. Being present and available to the people of God is so important, and this is a truly practical way to do that, and to make them feel like they matter, they count.

I have mostly positive feelings and memories of my seminary days. However, I have often said that it isn't the seminary that teaches you to be a priest; it's the people of your first parish. I spent six years at that parish in Modesto and was blessed with the hospitality and openness of the people there. I was also fortunate in the two priests I worked with, who taught me a lot by the example of their diligence and spirituality. It's often the little things that tell you the differences between countries. Growing up, none of my friends would have known the age of our parents, or of any adults, for that matter. It's just something you weren't told and didn't ask. My first

84

day in this new parish, I visited all the classrooms of the school. After giving a brief autobiographical description, I paused in 5th grade and said: "Any questions?" A girl at the back put up her hand and asked: "How old are you?" I realized, there and then, that I was in a different country.

Not long after my arrival I began teaching soccer to the children in the school. They had never heard of it before, and took to it immediately, especially since, after teaching them, I would organize games between classes, which brought out their great American competitiveness. Youngsters in a Catholic school live in every geographical area of a city, so I begun getting calls from teachers and principals of various public schools, asking if I would come and teach their youngsters soccer. Which I did. Doing this was something I thought was positive, for two reasons. First, I loved soccer and thought it was a great game for young people, since everyone could play and it taught teamwork while not putting too much individual pressure on each kid. Secondly, it was a good way to present a positive image to the young people in public schools. For those who were Catholic, it gave them a chance to see me in a different role in addition to when I would visit their Sunday school classrooms or when they came to Mass. For those who weren't Catholic, and who didn't have the slightest idea what a priest was, it showed them a human side to our church.

At any rate, the sport became popular in these schools and there followed a groundswell to start a youth soccer league. It grew very rapidly, from 90 players in 1975 to 700 the year after, to 1300 in 1977 to 1800 in 78 and above 2000 the following year. It was quite a struggle to get coaches and referees and fields and equipment to keep up with the demand, but the Modesto Youth Soccer Association, as we called it, was truly blessed by having many dedicated and talented board members to guide it thru such a rapid expansion.

The summer of 1979 was an eventful one. In June, I became a U.S. citizen. In July I turned 30. In September I was transferred to my second parish, in Tracy. When I was ten years old, my Father begun subscribing to Time magazine, which I read from cover to cover. Therefore, I had always been interested in American politics. Since I had committed to spend the rest of my life serving the people of God in Stockton diocese, I decided I should become a citizen, since I believe in the democratic process and in voting in every election. At the time, you were required to have two sponsors, so I picked a perfectly balanced ticket from among my friends: a liberal Democrat and a conservative Republican. Ironically, my voting has been split about even between both parties in the 21 years since then. However, the major presidential candidates always petition me not to vote for them, since I have only voted for one winner in the five presidential elections so far - a .200 batting average wouldn't get me in the major leagues.

Turning 30 wasn't as traumatic as I thought it would be. Two couples organized a surprise party for me, and it was a surprise, with lots of people and numerous speeches and gag gifts. It was bittersweet because we knew, at that time, that I would be leaving to another parish and gathered around me that evening were so many people who had come to mean so much to me and I knew it was going to be very difficult to say goodbye to them. I have never found it easy to leave any parish, but you do form attachments in your first parish that never leave and it was difficult indeed to move. From time to time, younger priests have asked me if moving from any parish is ever easy and I have no hesitation in telling them no, it's not. However, as an associate pastor, as difficult as it is for one's heart, it is good for one's head to move, if for no other reason that, eventually, you will be made a head pastor and it's important to have had experiences in different kinds of parishes and with different priests. Each parish you serve in teaches you what to do, and what not to do, and that's all part of growing as a human being as well as growing as a priest.

Up to now I've been talking about my training and life as a priest, but what about God? Where does God fit into the equation?

My Faith In God

I have always been interested in astronomy. I remember so clearly when, at the age of seven, my Father took my five-year-old brother and me up the road on a clear night to watch Sputnik go overhead. It was an awesome experience. The more I learned about the heavens, the more we have discovered about the vastness of the universe, the more convinced I am that there truly is a God. It's always been amazing to me that there is this so-called conflict between science and religion. For so long it was almost taken for granted that if one was a person of science, it would take you away from God. I don't think anything could be further from the truth. The more we learn, through scientific study of the incredible complexities of nature, especially the more knowledge we gain about ourselves as human beings, the more we should be awestruck about the being who created this complexity in the first place. The more we learn that our sun in only one of billions of suns in our own galaxy, and that there are billions of other galaxies, the surer we must be of an infinite being that put this all together in the first place.

Because of the sheer vastness of God, it deeply saddens me that we humans try to put this Supreme Being in boxes of our own design. We search for ways to relate to God that make sense to us, and that is all for the good. But if we then try to force these ways on others, and persecute or ostracize or in any way make feel second-class, people who have different ways than ours to find God, that is clearly misguided and wrong. In one sense, there are as many ways to God as there are people on this earth. And if there's life out there on other planets in other solar systems, they have their own way to God. Let none of us be so presumptuous as to think ours is the only way to the wondrous Creator of this mind-boggling universe.

Each of us needs to search for our own way to God. For me, the way is Christianity. In writing these next paragraphs, I need to ascribe to God something that isn't part of this Supreme Being, at least not in the narrow way we define the word: a gender. Instead of using God every second word, I will use Him, He or His, only because it's less repetitive. I believe that God loves us so much that He wanted to be with us on this magnificent blue planet. Jesus came among us to live for us and to die for us and to show us how much we are loved by our Creator. By total obedience to the will of God, whom He so lovingly described as Abba, Father, Jesus taught us the way to worship and praise and show our gratitude to God on this earth and how to attain presence with Him in the life after our time on earth is over. When Jesus returned to the Father, he promised to send the Holy Spirit to be with us and guide us in our journey on Earth.

In essence, the teachings of Christ are simple and pure. It is a great sadness that people have fought over them for two thousand years. If we remember that the reason for Jesus coming was to show us God's love for us and to guide us to the Father, we should be satisfied when someone discovers that love and that way, instead of arguing and disputing about interpretations of this passage or that from scripture or elsewhere. Fundamentally, the core of Christianity is belief in the Trinity, the Father, Son and Holy Spirit. It's understandable that people of faiths other than Christianity, which have a different approach to God, would have arguments with us about our approach. But since all Christian churches profess the same core belief, we shouldn't harbor resentments or issue condemnations of those within Christianity who don't go exactly along with the way we see things.

I have been a member of various ministerial associations or groups in every community where I have been stationed. I believe it's important to have fellowship with the ministers of other churches and denominations. It's always heartening to discover, over and over again, that our similarities of belief far surpass whatever differences we might have. One of the discoveries I have made is how many members of fundamental bible churches totally misunderstand statues and sacred paintings in Catholic churches. This was really brought home to me in my first parish, when a new, non-denominational congregation asked if they could use our church building for a Sunday night service. I was helping them set up their sound equipment when one of the workers said to me "Would you mind if we moved the idol so can put our speaker there?" He was referring to a statue of Mary, Jesus' Mother. He didn't mean any offense by the question; obviously, to him, Catholics worship statues, so this was an idol.

Of course we don't worship statues, or paintings or anything else except for God, no more than the people who constructed the statues of Lincoln and Jefferson in Washington D.C. worship those statues and no more than people who have photos of their families on their desk worship the photos. They are just a reminder to us of scenes from the life of Jesus, or the lives of saints who have lived their lives as closely as they could to the teachings of Christ. However, I do think we can learn from other Christian churches how best to portray these scenes and figures. An example that springs to mind is that of Mary, the Mother of Jesus. I really admire the artwork of Orthodox Churches, who often have icons of Mary, but always with the Christ child present. A reminder to us that Mary's glory was in her being the Christ-bearer, and that she should always be thought of in that reflection.

Let me now end where I began, as a Tipperary boy, and please join me as we pray together in the Irish tradition.

AN IRISH PRAYER

I have been honored to be part of this book, which explores people's lives, at the same time as it looks at different approaches to God. The best stage production I have ever seen is the musical "Les Miserables" and my favorite line from that show comes near the end: "To love another person is to see the face of God". Our challenge and privilege in our journey through life is to see God's face everywhere, and especially in His gift of love, which can conquer all adversity. In exploring our various approaches to God, let us always do so in the spirit of God's all-conquering love for us.

In conclusion, here is a traditional Irish blessing prayer:

> **May the roads rise up to meet you**
> **May the winds be ever at your back**
> **May the sun shine warm upon your face**
> **May the rains fall soft upon your fields**
> **And, until we meet again**
> **May God hold you in the hollow of His hand**

10

FINDING GOD IN EDGEMONT

None of us live our religion in the abstract; we all pursue it, flee from it, or simply ignore it in the muddled process called life. Much of my "muddling-up" came during the teenage years in Edgemont.

An eccentric friend of mine, carrying a bed roll, walked from New York to California, wearing out a half-dozen pairs of shoes in the process. I never understood what motivated his trip, but he did receive a good education along the way in the trivia of America. On his return he told me this:

"Regardless of how desolate the country I walked through, whether the coal fields of Pennsylvania, endless flat plains of Kansas, or a desert prairie of Nevada, the local people always told me the same thing, "We are lucky to live in this town; it is such a great place, and I can't imagine being as happy living any place else."

I'm not sure that was true of Edgemont where I lived during my difficult teenage years.

Edgemont sits on the banks of the Cheyenne River at the southern edge of the Black Hills where the sage brush prairie rolls south toward Nebraska. There isn't much left of the town anymore. Half the business district was burnt to the ground a couple decades ago and never rebuilt, because most of the buildings were already abandoned, mostly World War Two saloons whose patrons were long gone. A few homes with green lawns remain, but most are run-down and others unoccupied. Our former home site is now a vacant lot- not a great loss - it was a barely livable relic we found to live in during the war-time boom years. Sunflowers now struggle there in the hot summer sun. Edgemont is a "boom town" that has gone to "bust".

Edgemont filled my teen years and I am still unable to place it in perspective. There were some good times to fondly remember, and others I'd just as soon forget. I suppose everyone's teen years have ups and downs. When several of my former classmates have gotten together in recent years, we talk about the "good old days," and how great they were. It is a blessing to live long enough that the bad times begin to disappear, and the good times rise to the top.

There was a very personal aspect to my life in Edgemont that I do not share with my classmates at our reunions. It is when I found God. Until then I had only been going through the motions of a religious faith. A prayer was something I recited by rote, usually while thinking of something else, or wishing I was some place else. Then something unique happened to me as a teenager in Edgemont and I'm not sure even to this day what caused it: I began to feel the presence of a God.

Perhaps it was the personal influence of some new buddies who were true believers. Or it may have been due to my new pastor, Father Groell, a strange and unapproachable cleric, but a devout Christian who gave sermons that were truly inspiring. Or maybe the greatest impact came from my new role as an altar boy. I wasn't just sitting out there in the church as a spectator on a hard pew, but I was up at the altar actively participating with the priest in the service. For the first time in my life this ancient religious pageant of the Mass came alive for me. When the priest consecrated the bread and wine into the body and blood of Christ, there was absolutely no doubt in my mind but that our God was physically present with us. For the first time in my life, I would even pray directly to him as I kneeled at the altar.

At this time I was learning Latin in school, so I began to understand the liturgy of the Mass. The ultimate challenge for an altar boy was to learn the Confiteor. In those days, everything in the Catholic Mass except the sermon was in Latin or Greek.

Confiteor Deo omnipotenti,
Beatae Mariae, semper Virgini,
Beato Michaeli Archangelo,
Beato Joanni Baptistae,
Sanctis Apostolis Petro et Paulo,
omnibus Sanctis et tibe,Pater,
quia peccavi nimis cogitatione, verbo,
et opere,
mea culpa, mea culpa, mea maxima culpa.

Ideo precor
Beatam Mariam semper Virginem ....

I even knew what this prayer meant. Confiteor is the Latin for "I confess." I confessed my sins to Blessed Mary ever virgin, St. Michael, and the others; mea culpa's were an admission that it was through my fault, through my fault, through my most grievous fault; then the last half of the prayer, when everything ended with "m" instead of "o", a change from objective to subjective voice, was a plea for all those same people to pray for me.

We altar boys said The Confiteor in a low mumble while kneeling beside the priest, and it was easy to fake the prayer if we remembered three things: start with a loud "Confiteor Deo"; then lower the voice to a mumble; hit the "Mea Culpa's" loudly as you pound the breast as a sign of self humiliation; and then end with a pious sounding "Dominium Deum Nostrum." That is how the priest said it.

There were some burdens to bear as a Catholic, and that is true in all religious faiths. I couldn't eat meat on Friday, which was no big deal at home, but it was a pain-in-the-rear when I was out in public, particularly for school events. Either someone had to make a fuss to get a fish meal scheduled so we Catholics could be included, or I had to abstain from the main course, or I had to quietly pretend that I forget it was Friday and eat whatever was served. Of course there was usually some Methodist sitting next to me to remind me it was Friday. In those days the Vatican decreed that it was a mortal sin to eat meat on Friday, and if not confessed with appropriate penance from a priest, it meant an everlasting damnation to the fires of Hell. I qualified for dozens of those fires, but I'm not sure I ever accepted that the punishment fit the crime. Could God be that cruel? Fortunately for me, my sin slate was wiped clean at the time of Vatican Two, when the Friday meat ban was quietly dropped.

Then there was the more serious social issue of intermarriage. I think almost everyone would agree that a marriage of two people with the same religious faith, all other things being equal, is the best avenue for a successful marriage. Since my father and mother entered into a mixed marriage and had a happy union until the day my father died 47 years later, a mixed religious combination can work, however, it was no bed of roses. My father was never well accepted by his in-laws, because their daughter was forced to make a pledge to the church to raise us kids as Catholic. The church discouraged all such marriages and would not permit the ceremony to be celebrated with a Nuptial Mass. Those impediments were some serious considerations for young people who were dating and shopping around for a spouse. The end result was that anyone from another religion would seldom marry a Catholic, and genuine Catholics would not marry someone that would cause themselves to be ex-communicated. I was rather shy and found it difficult to muster the courage to ask a girl for a date anyway, so religious impediments were very high hurdles. It seemed the only girls I was ever interested in were Protestants, and the religious thing was always there.

Now as I look back at that time in my young life, I wonder how such a genuine faith in a supreme being could be re-generated again. Maybe there is a naiveté that comes with youth, or conversely a built-in cynicism that develops with age. Thank God, I was able to drink from that well at least once in my life.

11

ISLAM

"The religious faith of Muslims, based on the words and religious system founded by the prophet Muhammad in the sixth century AD in Mecca and taught by the Koran, the basic principle of which is absolute submission to the unique and personal god, Allah."

About 600 years after the Christian faith was started in the Holy Land, another religious faith, Islam, was started nearby in the desert of what is now Saudia Arabia. Until recent years few Americans could have told you anything about this religion, and even now many know about it only in reference to the World Trade Center disaster. I had never heard of it in my youth, but have now had considerable exposure to Muslims in my business and travel to Bahrain, Egypt, Malaysia, Bosnia, Morocco, and Indonesia. The more I know about Islam, the more respect I have for the peoples of this religion.

Even after twenty years of association with Muslims and a study of their religion, I may not truly understand Islam, nor able to explain it to others; it seems a beautiful religious faith, but differs from our western culture. Those of us from the west also start with hostility, since it is diffi-cult to distinguish between the Islamic religious faith and the political re-gimes of Iraq, Iran, the Ottoman Empire, or the extremist Taliban fanatics of Afghanistan. Much of this started with the storming of the American embassy during the Iranian revolution, the invasion by Iraq during the Gulf War, and then the World Trade Center disaster; but branding the Islamic religion with this political legacy is as unfair as calling Christians barbarians because of their history during the Crusades, the Spanish Inquisition, or even more recently in Northern Ireland or Rowanda. Prior to the New York disaster of 9/11, the worse terrorist event in American history was the Oklahoma City bombing that was perpetrated by Timothy McVey, who was raised a Catholic; an hour before his death asked to receive last rites from a Catholic Priest; yet it is not fair to brand the Catholic faith with the disaster he created. Likewise, it is not fair to blame the Islamic faith because of the terrorism of Osama Bin Laden and other fanatics.

While over twenty percent of the world's populations are Muslim, most Americans know nothing about the Islamic religious faith, nor have any personal contact with a Muslim. With apologies to my Muslim friends for any unintended inaccuracies concerning their religion, let me begin with my first association with Islam.

I had no contact with the Islamic faith until mid-life when my youngest daughter became an exchange student and was assigned to live in Surabaya, Indonesia with a family that was Islamic. In preparation for the trip she asked me to explain their religion. I knew absolutely nothing to tell her. We bid her good-bye and sent her onward to Indonesia. Months later she returned, and her knowledge and respect for the Islamic faith had grown immensely. Her heritage as a Catholic served her well in a Muslim family, particularly her respect for their religious traditions such as kneeling in prayer several times a day. Without flaunting their religion, they were very devout. She also had the unique experience of wearing the Muslim robe and attending prayer services with her family in an Islamic mosque. She returned to our Catholic home with great respect for the Islamic religious faith.

In subsequent years I had considerable exposure to Muslims with business that took me to several Muslim nations. My first encounter was in Jakarta, Indonesia. I arrived late at night and climbed into bed. During the night I was awakened several times by the prayer of a Muezzin (Muslim crier) from the minaret of a nearby mosque, reciting the call that summoned the faithful to prayer. This was during the season of Ramadan, when a Muslim must fast from sunup to sunset, and occurs during the ninth month of the Muslim calendar to commemorate when the Koran was revealed to Muhammad. The plant manager, Mohammed Isad, met me at the hotel, and we drove to his factory in the outskirts of Jakarta. We were acquainted from his previous visits to my office in the United States. He was Muslim. After spending several days in his factory, where I was helping with some quality issues, we became good friends. On the last day of my visit, I got the courage to ask if I could attend a mosque with him. He obliged, and together we walked to the mosque. Removing our shoes at the entrance, we entered a large room full of men sitting on the floor. The chanting began, and then all the men dropped to their knees and lowered their heads to the floor in prayer. I did likewise. Being somewhat intimidated by the scene, I must confess that my prayer was mostly for safe passage from Jakarta. We arose in the tightly packed sea of humanity, and left the mosque. As we walked back to the hotel he explained some aspects of his religious faith. Like most Catholics, he seemed to know only bits and pieces of the history, and some of what he said sounded more like a tradition, something he inherited from his culture. In that respect he was no different from most the rest of us who also inherited our religion.

During the years in my job, I had business dealings with many others of the Islamic faith, and we often shared our mutual respect for the other's religion. It was explained to me over lunch by an Egyptian factory manager that Muhammad was a great prophet and a messenger from their God, Allah; He was the last of the great prophets, preceded by Abraham, Moses, and Jesus. A Muslim sees Christianity and Judaism as a part of Islam, and the Jewish Jehovah and Christian Yahweh are only different names for the same God, Allah. Islam completes the earlier revelations around which the Christian and Jewish faiths were built, and corrects human misinterpretation of these earlier revelations. For example, Muslims believe that Jesus was a prophet second only to Muhammad in importance, but his followers later introduced into Christianity the heretical idea that Jesus was the Son of God. So while they consider Christianity and Judaism as parts of the Islamic faith, both these religious faiths were lead astray by heretical beliefs interjected by followers in later years.

The story of Muhammad is difficult for us to comprehend, since it took place in the Arabic culture which is so different from the one we know. The attitudes and cultural mores we inherited from our European ancestry are so indoctrinated into our psychic that we must place ourselves psychologically into another world before we can understand how an Arabian named Muhammad, who spent his youth plodding the desert in caravans from Arabia to Syria, could establish the greatest religion in the world in terms of numbers of believers, the religious fervor of followers, and its potential impact on the world. In the west we refer to Muhammad's youth spent in caravans as a means of ridicule, inferring that an illiterate wanderer could hardly converse with God. We overlook the role an itinerant carpenter from Nazareth named Jesus played in the Christian religion.

As a young man Muhammad lived in the city of Mecca in what is now Saudi Arabia. There were two cities in that area, Medina and Mecca, and they were cultural and business rivals. Both had been little more than watering holes for the Arabic tribes for centuries. During the period of 400 AD, there was a large immigration of Jews who were being driven out of Syria and Palestine into Arabia. This new Jewish population was well received, and their industry helped both Medina and Mecca prosper and grow into cities, supporting populations of about 20,000 each. The Jewish men joined the military and fought side by side with Arabs against invading Christian armies. This was a time when the Jews and Arabs lived together in peace.

Within this climate, Muhammad was born in Mecca in 519 AD, losing both parents before the age of six, and he was raised by relatives. As a youth he was a shepherd boy and later joined the caravans that crossed the desert to Yemen and Syria. At the age of twenty-five he married a wealthy, forty-five year old widow with whom he lived for a quarter century. After the death of this wife, when he was fifty-one, he took several wives in his later life.

In mid-life, Muhammad had a dream. It was to unite the warring tribes of his people, to give them a unified religion, and to raise them to an honored position in the world. This dream was to become a reality. The critical encounter was similar to that of Abraham and Moses. It took place in a cave in the desert when Muhammad was forty; God manifested himself to Muhammad in the form of the angel Gabriel. The angel showed him a tablet which he could read by God's revelation, since until that instant he was illiterate. The tablet stated that Allah, the true God, had appointed Muhammad to be his messenger on earth. Muslims place great emphasis on the fact that Muhammad until this moment was illiterate and instantly received the gift of literacy from Allah, and was then able to record the message of the Koran. This is equated with the virgin birth of Jesus, another of their prophets, who received the miraculous birth as a gift from the God, Allah.

Afterwards, Muhammad told this story to his family and friends, but belief was slow in coming. Like the Christians before him, the first converts were slaves, but the Arab population viewed him with suspicion - a radical. After ten years the bitterness against him in Mecca grew among the aristocracy, and he fled to Medina. Many of his followers had preceded him to Medina, and there he was welcomed as a Prophet. This migration is known as the Hegura, and is honored among Muslims by the dating of their calendar from that event.

The Koran came into existence as a revelation to Muhammad from Allah. This is the holy book of Muslims, written in Arabic, and it means "a reading" or "a recital". The first Koran utterances that were revealed to Muhammad were memorized or written on palm leaves or tablets of stone. To a Muslim, the Koran is not a man-made book. It is divine, uncreated, the manifest voice of the Deity. The Koran stresses the unity and sovereignty of God. It is a literary masterpiece which mirrors the psychological, social, and economic aspects of Arabic life, as well as moral and spiritual elements.

The Koran is difficult reading for non-Arabic. A spirit of dignified grandeur permeates the whole of the book in a format we are not familiar with from our western literature, and the arrangement of chapters runs almost contrary to our traditional chronological sequence. Nevertheless, the immense influence of the Koran upon the development of the later Arabic style makes this work a cornerstone not only of their religion, but also of their literature.

For a time in Medina, Muhammad turned to the Jewish population for support, hoping they would recognize him as the Prophet successor to Moses and Jesus. When they rejected him, he turned against them and waged a battle to take their wealth.

He also raided the caravans of Mecca. As his wealth grew he became able to raise a large army. Hostilities developed between Mecca and Medina, and Muhammad was the victor. Within a few years he ruled all of Arabia. As his political power increased, so also his Islamic religion spread.

Soon thereafter, Muhammad died in 632 at the age of sixty-two. If it were not for a friend who picked up the mantle, the Islamic creed may have died with him. The friend, Abu Behr, became the successor. Whereas Muhammad had been the Prophet who delivered the creed, it was Abu Behr who used the sword to carry the Koran to the outside world. While his name is scarcely known to Westerners, he was one of the giants of history. Because of him, the Arab nomads of the sixth century became the conquerors of many foreign lands. By the eighth century they ruled an empire that covered all sides of the Mediterranean. My Shiite Muslim friends do not agree with this assessment of the important role of Abu Behr documented by some historians, as I will discuss later.

Never before had a single idea created, in terms of conquest and culture, an impact such as the religion given to the world by Muhammad. Christianity, the other great moving force, had in a thousand years won to its teachings only a few lands of Western Europe. On the other hand, in the space of one hundred years following the death of Muhammad, the Arabs had carried the sword of Islam from the Atlantic to the Indian Ocean, holding at one time Syria, Persia, Egypt, North Africa, the Holy Land, Armenia, Afghanistan, a third of India, and much of Spain.

They came with the sword, but they retained the best of what they discovered. Much of what we know of the very considerable Arab science was born of the minds of Jews, Persians, Greeks, various central Asian peoples, and the Berbers, but it flowered under Arab protection, impelled by Arab enthusiasm. "A scholar was welcome everywhere and might travel thousands of miles through Muslim lands, welcomed in each city by a sultan, bey, or emir, presented with gifts, honored, escorted, entertained, and above all listened to with attention." As their supply lines lengthened, their expansion was ultimately stopped in France.

When I visited Seville, Spain, which has Muslim, Byzantine, Jewish, and Christian roots, I was confused by the architecture of its Roman Catholic cathedral, which claimed to be the third largest in the world after St. Peters in Rome and St. Pauls in London. The cathedral did not have the basilica structure I was familiar with from the cathedrals of Western Europe. Then I learned it was originally built as an Islamic Mosque. After the Christians drove the Muslims out of Spain, they tore off the mosque roof, replacing it with the familiar cathedral superstructure and flying buttresses. Spain offers many opportunities to see remnants of a former Islamic empire. Cordoba was capital of Islamic Spain from the 8th to 11th centuries, and during the 10th century was the largest city in Europe. Granada, with the beautiful Alhambra palace of the Caliph, was the last stronghold of Islam in Western Europe and fell to the Christian ruler, Elizabeth in 1485 - the same time she was negotiating with Columbus for his exploration to the new world.

By 1000 AD, the Islamic empire had reached its zenith and gradually crumbled over the next several centuries. Part became fragmented into Sultanates and Caliphates. The Crusaders attacked from Europe as they fought toward the holy land. The Mongols under Genghes Khan then invaded from the East, and in the first battle between Moslem and Mongol an army of 400,000 Moslems was defeated and all killed. Can you imagine that scene? When Baghdad capitulated to the Mongols, 800,000 Muslim civilians were killed, then the city lay waste. Ultimately, the Mongols were stopped in Egypt in 1303 AD. In the aftermath of the Mongolian empire collapse, the new Muslim Ottoman Empire gradually came into existence out of Turkey. This empire survived for several centuries until its collapse during World War One.

While the Muslim political empire collapsed, not so the Islamic religious faith. Not only has it survived, but is today the world's largest religion. Although exact statistics are not available, the Muslim world population is estimated at more than one and a third billion.

What is there about the Islamic faith that has claimed such a fervent following for so many centuries through so many parts of the world? Perhaps the answer is found in the spirit of brotherhood that Muslims feel with a simple religious message that appeals to the common instincts. Against it were pitted Judaism which was based on a racial theme, and Christianity which preached of Trinities, doctrines, and heresies that ordinary man could not make heads or tails of.

Muslims do not worship Muhammad, their Prophet, but regard him as God's messenger. And what was God's message? Here are the five affirmations of Islam from the time of Muhammad, and they remain unchanged now 1500 years later:

ONE: **"Allahu akbar", Allah is great. He is a merciful and compassionate ruler of the universe.**

TWO: **There are rewards and punishments awaiting in a hereafter - either a paradise, or an eternal fire.**

THREE: **Muhammad was God's messenger, to convey his revelation**

FOUR: **The Koran is a revelation by Allah.**

FIVE: **The Brotherhood of Islam includes all who reverence Allah, His Prophet, Book, and the Day of Judgment.**

The basic duties of Muslims, the "pillars of Islam", were revealed in the Koran. They are the belief that there is one God, and it is the people's duty to believe in him and serve him in the manner he laid out in the Koran; they are required to kneel in prayer five times a day; must give charity to help those poorer than themselves; must fast during the month of Ramadan; and must make a pilgrimage (Hajj) at least once during their lifetime. Islam is a Theistic religion that acknowledged the validity of Judaism and Christianity, believing it to be the fulfillment of those two earlier religions. They consider Moses and Christ to be Prophets, as predecessors to their Prophet,

Muhammad - who is the last Prophet from their God, Allah. They made decisive breaks with these prior religions, substituting Friday for the Sabbath, and eventually proclaiming Mecca to be the center of religious faith.

The basic Islamic doctrine is that Allah is the supreme being; He is the beginning and the end; every aspect of existence is present in Him; He is the Creator and the law giver; He is a supernatural reality and does not possess an earthly manifestation; and God cannot be represented in an worldly form (which has discouraged the representational arts in Islam). Another key doctrine is that of prophesy. Muslims believe that prophesy lies at the heart of human history, beginning with Adam as the first prophet and ending with Muhammad as the last. Man is the servant of God. By surrendering to the will of God, man finds salvation and peace.

What appeals to a Muslim was that his God, Allah, was a righteous God they could understand; that acceptance of his doctrine opened the door to the brotherhood of trustworthy men on earth; and to a paradise in the hereafter. This came without any ambiguous symbolism, or darkening of altars, or chanting of priests.

As someone raised in a western Christian culture, my ability to accurately describe the Islamic faith is inadequate. I have relied on references from encyclopedias and history books, but these were all written by westerners, and my Muslim friends tell me such books do not catch the essence, nor reveal the true meaning of the Islamic Faith. With an apology to my Muslim friends for any inaccuracies, I have utilized the same secular references used for my look at other religions.

It seems that all religions encounter the splintering into different sects, and such is also the case with Islam. While there is only one Islamic religion based on the Koran, by the tenth century, Islam had ceased to be one empire, having two distinct divisions. The schism that divided the Muslim world into two camps began only a few years after the death of Muhammad. When he died he left no clear instructions either designating a successor or setting up a system by which leaders could be chosen.

The sect known as "Sunnites" chose Abu Behr, Muhammad's closest companion, as leader. The Sunnites, recognized by many as the traditional

Islamic religion, today represents 65% of all Muslims. Except for Iran, their religion is nearly world-wide.

Another important sect is the Ibadites, whose followers are to be found in parts of Arabia, along the eastern coast of Africa, and in North Africa. They form a separate community in Islam, but differ little with the Sunnites. There are also a couple dozen other smaller sects scattered through the Muslim world, mostly confined to a region or country.

The sect known as "Shiites" supported the claim of Ali Bin Abi Toleb, Mohammad's son-in-law, to become the caliph (or leader). They feel called upon to restore the true teachings and ethical principles of the original Islam. Shiism grew to be more mystical in orientation; to believe in the intercession of saints on behalf of God; emphasizes mercy over justice; and faith over good works. Shiism also developed more fully a class of religious scholars to interpret the law for the faithful. The most senior of these are popularly known as Ayatollahs, "Signs of God".   Americans are familiar with the late Ayatollah Kohomeni of Iran. Today, the Shiites represent 10% of all Muslims and are found principally in Iran and Bahrain, with significant minorities in Kuwait, the UAE, and Saudi Arabian's Eastern Providence.

Recently, my wife and I visited Bahrain, a Muslim island nation of the Arabian Gulf, living with our daughter and family in the local community. During the visit I developed friendships with several Bahraini. One of them, a handsome Persian, is the owner of a Persian carpet store. Born and raised in Iran, he is a Shiite Muslim and quite knowledgeable and devout in his Islamic religion. He is fluent in English, speaks several languages, well read, and is a brilliant conversationalist. When my wife pursued the Persian carpet world with his employees, he served me tea while we talked religion and Middle East politics. He observed that the people of most nations are victims of the propaganda from their own government, and examples of this are the cultural clashes between Western Culture and that of the Middle East. As a result, each side harbors prejudices against the religions and national politics of the other. Case in point: differences between the United States and Iran.

First, the American view of Iran during the last half of the 20th century. The late Shah of Iran was a fine man and a loyal friend of the United States. He grew to love our country and came often to vacation, to date Hollywood movie stars, to pursue his passion for fast cars, and for medical checkups. His air force officers were trained in the United States, and one of his hobbies was to fly American fighter jets. He took a somewhat secular view of religion and de-emphasized the role of the Muslim Shiite religion in his country, encouraging western dress and a relaxed lifestyle that permitted the youth to frequent movies and discos. At the time of the anniversary of his monarchy, he threw a lavish week-long party at his palace in Teheran at which the President of the United States (Carter) and First Lady were honored guests. Not coincidentally, he also made Iranian oil readily available at nominal prices to the American market that was thirsty for foreign oil. The mutual support between the Shah or Iran and the American government was seen as in our "best national interests".

Now for the very different Iranian view of the Shah and this relationship with America that lead to the Iranian Revolution of 1979.   U n t i l the mid-1920's, Iran had a stable government under a semi-democratic monarch when the Riza Shah Pahlavi family came to power through a coup d'etat. In 1941, with the abdication of the Riza Shah, the Shah Pahlavi came to power. His premier, Dr. Mohammad Mossadegh lead a stable government, but one that attempted to assert Iran control over Iran oil rather than leaving it under foreigners. This lead to conflict with the Shah, who dismissed Mossadegh, then in 1954 had him arrested.   He then tilted politically toward American and allowed the Iranian oil resources to flow overseas. The Shah maintained a ruthless regime. All political dissents were thrown in jail, and few emerged again. Jails had torture chambers that rivaled those of the Ottoman Empire and Turks. It became a police state. His secret police rivaled the Gestapo in intrigue, torture, and political repression. The Muslim religious leader, Ayatollah Kohomeni, fled into exile to France where for a decade he led a dissident campaign. Finally, in 1979 the repressive regime of the Shah developed some vulnerability when the Shah developed cancer and went to the United States for treatment. When the Ayatollah suddenly returned from Exile to Iran, a spontaneous uprising of the people of Iran against the Shah forced him to flee the country, and he died soon after from cancer. As in most such movements, a near anarchy developed and there were political excesses as one wave of revolutionaries replaced another. The American embassy was stormed, and the occupants taken as hostage, since they were seen as conspirators with the Shah. Gradually over the years, the revolutionary movement stabilized. Today, Iran is the only democracy in the Middle East. It has an elected parliament that makes laws, although certain religious groups do have a degree of veto power. It has an independent judiciary. It has a president who is freely elected. It has a Muslim population that is true to their Shiite religious practice as taught by the Koran. While the religious leaders are a powerful factor, they do not hold total control over the political process or government. There are, unfortunately, zealots within Iran who practice terrorism in the same manner as both sides pursue terrorist activities in the Arab-Israel conflict, the Northern Ireland conflict, and even in the martial arms cells of Oklahoma City, USA. But the fact remains; Iran is a near-democracy, and perhaps an evolving role model for some other countries of the Middle East.

Which of these two views of Iran are more accurate? The answer for any individual may depend on the prejudices one brings from their culture of the East or the West.

I also developed a second friendship in Bahrain with a neighbor, Abdullah, also a Shiite Muslim. He was married and father of five children. With the meager salary of only 100 deniers per month (about $270) he found it difficult to maintain a bare subsistence for his family. He invited me to his home. It was a spartan apartment, clean yet sparsely furnished. His hospitable wife made a brief appearance to serve tea as we reclined on a carpet, and his children watched from the corner. They were happy looking children and spoke English, a required subject for all Bahraini children starting in the fourth grade. They were eager to talk with an American, using their newly-learned language. The happy, yet spartan scene reminded me of my youth during the depression years in South Dakota, where my family lived under nearly identical circumstances. I talked religion with Abdullah, trying to better understand Islam. He was quick to explain that while there are Sunnites and Shiites, there is only one Islamic religion, and that is based on their scared book, the Koran. It teaches them religion. They all go to their Mosque and chant the same prayers from the Koran. As I said goodbye to Abdullah and his family, I felt I had begun to better understand that beneath our two cultures there was a common ground in which all peoples and religious faiths can find friendship with each other.

I have been in Islamic mosque in Europe, Africa, the Middle East, and Asia. Although there is one in a nearby town here in California, I have never attended services there, but someday I intend to. Religious etiquette requires worshipers to remove their shoes before entering the sanctuary. Modest dress is expected, including head covering for all women. Men and women sit separately in the sanctuary; both sit on the floor when not standing or kneeling for prayer. Visitors are expected to stand when others do, but not to kneel or bow   Islam has learned doctors, teachers, muezzins, and preachers, but no priests.

If I had been aware of the depth of the Islamic religious experience twenty-five years ago, I'm not sure I would have had the courage to let my teenage daughter climb on that plane all by herself headed to Indonesia to live with Muslims. But then think of what she would have missed; and for myself, as an urban cowboy aboard jets riding fence lines around the world, I have learned to appreciate much about the fine Islamic culture.

12

RIDING THE FENCE LINES

By S. Amjad Hussain

The prairies of South Dakota where Bernie Keating grew up and the narrow streets and alleys of Peshawar in northwest Pakistan where I had my upbringing have apparently nothing in common. In terms of distance these two places at the opposite side of the world are eons apart. But here I am, a hyphenated American, living in American Midwest identifying with an urban cowboy. What links both of us, and millions of other people like us, is a commonality of purpose of our individual lives. It is a quest, often unrecognized, to find spirituality in places that we never thought we would find. We all ride life fences stocked with our own special provisions and equipped with our own unique tools. In the end our destination, I firmly believe, is the same. We all reach home even if through different routes and taking different paths.

During our life journeys we constantly encounter mysterious loose ends that lead us to new vistas and occasionally to dead ends. As we travel on the vast expanses of unmarked and uncharted land that is strewn with land mines of self-doubt and false gods of dogma, rituals and traditions we try to understand the world around us and in the process we discover ourselves.

All religions are good and noble. They are supposed to help us cope with myriad problems and issues that we face every day in our lives. These issues are more practical and near than those surrounding our salvation. These mundane, down to earth, issues deal with family relations, societal responsibility, collusion between personal interests and those of the community or society. They also make us understand the difference between individual and collective responsibility for the disfranchised and the casts-away of the society. It would be easy if we sit out our lives, as some people are prone to do, in a secluded prairie cabin without venturing out on life trails. For such people, a minority I presume, the conflict between the temporal and the eternal can wait. The rest have to venture out and face these conflicts and learn from them.

What follows is the account of my personal journey through life as a practicing Muslim.

A humble start

I was born in the walled city of Peshawar along the northwest frontier of what before 1947 was British India and is now Pakistan. I grew up amidst an extended family of 30 to 35 members in a quiet neighborhood. In our ancestral home, a rambling relic from mid 19th century, my mother, five brothers, three sisters, four aunts, and an assortment of cousins, relatives, perennial guests and a few servants lived. My father had died when I was six and financial burden of supporting a large household fell on the shoulders of my four half brothers. Those brothers, much older than me, played a pivotal role in my education and my upbringing.

Religion was very much part of our lives and so was laughter and gaiety. We lived religion in the most relaxed and fun way. Since no newspaper came to our house, an old Grundig short-wave radio was the only link between the women of the household and the outside world. We would all eagerly await the music programs and the sound of popular Indian and Pakistani movie music wafted over the neighborhood. Older folks read the Qura'n and prayed five times a day as required of all believers. The younger generation did the same but not with any regularity. Though religion was also taught in school, we absorbed much of it from our surroundings.

Pillars and Posts

The religion of Islam is based on five well-defined pillars that have remained solid and definite ever since the start of the religion 1400-year ago. These include belief in one God and in the prophecy of prophet Muhammad, to pray five times a day at appointed hours, to observe absolute fast from dawn to dusk for one month every year in the holy month of Ramadan, to pay two and one half percent of one's savings in charity and finally to perform pilgrimage to Mecca at least once in one's lifetime provided one can afford it and has no overriding family obligations.

Islam reveres all the prophets of the Old Testament and their scriptures and reinforces the Mosaic laws. It considers Jesus as a great prophet and reaffirms Immaculate Conception. These beliefs, in addition to the five pillars, are integral part of the faith and are *sine qua non* for a Muslim.

The fountainhead of Islam is Qura'n, the holy book. It is the compilations of divine revelations that Prophet Muhammad received over 23- years. It is the cornerstone of Islamic civilization and the source of everything Islamic. *Sharia* or the Islamic law takes its authority not only from the *Qura'n* but also from *Sunnah*, the recorded sayings and deeds of the Prophet. In terms of authority, *Sunnah* is considered complimentary to the *Qura'n* and has the force of law only in areas where the *Qura'n* does not provide a clear direction. In the northwest corner of British India where I grew up *Qura'n* and *Sunnah* was the guiding force in our lives. It provided guidance, spiritual fulfillment and answers to all problems from mundane to profound.

The *Qura'n* was revealed to the Prophet in Arabic and according to Muslim traditions we were required to read it in Arabic even though we did not understand the language. From generation to generation it was passed down in a unique way by the women in our household. The neighborhood children would come to our home in the afternoon to learn the reading of the *Qura'n* the meaning of which neither the teachers nor the students knew.

The five obligatory prayers were also offered in Arabic. When the muezzin chanted the call for prayers from the corner mosque, the men would

111

head to the mosque whereas the women, after performing the ritual ablution, would set up prayer mats in the direction of Mecca and bow their heads in prayer. Those of us who skipped the ritual would be gently reminded of our obligation to pray but never forced into it.

During Ramadan, the month long period of absolute fasting from dawn to dusk, our daily routine would change drastically. Since Islamic practices follow the lunar calendar, Ramadan comes ten days early every year and thus in time s35des ahead from season to season. Summers were the hardest to fast because of 16-hours long days. Unbearable heat and unquenchable thirst took its toll from all of us. In the winter months it was rather easy.

While we could be lax in our five daily prayers, the fasting in Ramadan was observed rather rigidly. At age ten the children were expected to fast at least part of the day to help them develop self-control. By age fourteen they were required to observe full fast. A child's or teenager's first fast was celebrated as a memorable landmark by the entire family.

During Ramadan we all got up at three in the morning to eat a freshly prepared meal and drink plenty of fluids. At sunset the entire family would gather to break the fast at the sound of a siren or the boom of a cannon. Late evenings were spent in the neighborhood mosque for special Ramadan prayers. During my childhood and adolescence Ramadan was special because of the family meals and the much-anticipated boom of the cannon at sunset. With age the spiritual dimensions have became more central to food or pageantry. At the end of the month long period of fasting, we celebrated the festival of *Eid-ul-Fitr* one of the two main holidays. As children we would receive the gift of money which we eagerly spent in the festival that was held on such occasion just outside the city.

The family observed the forth pillar of Zakat or the annual alms giving rather quietly. The elders would calculate as to how much money needed to be given and without fanfare the amount was given to the poor in the neighborhood and to some members of the extended family. Occasionally part of the money was spent to help some poor parents marry off their daughter.

The last of the five pillars, the pilgrimage to Mecca was the least observed during my childhood. In the forties not many people either had the means or the ease of travel to make the arduous journey to Mecca. Only the very rich or the old undertook the long journey. The older people were probably driven by their desire to breathe their last in the Holy Land and to be buried there. The returning pilgrim was called Hajj or Hajis and given a rousing welcome by the family, friends and neighbors, their return was celebrated as a community event. As air travel became more feasible and accessible more and more people at a younger age started going for Hajj or the pilgrimage.

We absorbed religion by seeing it practiced in our surroundings. We did not learn it as much from boring schoolbooks or from listening to un-inspiring sermons in the mosque. The streets, alleys and neighborhoods were the real teachers where we imbibed the essence and the essentials.

One of my vivid memories from my childhood is my mother starting her day by reciting the Qura'n. She would get up at the crack of dawn, perform the ritual ablution and perform her early morning prayers. She would then take the Qura'n from the niche in the bedroom wall, lay it open on a pillow and sit cross- legged on the bed. I would crawl close to her and put my head in her lap while she read the book in a subdued chant in the early morning light filtering in through a slightly open window. When she would finish she would blow the blessings on my face and on all others who slept in the small room on the floor. Years later when I was struggling in a hospital bed after a heart attack, I had recurrent dreams of lying in her lap listening to her reciting the Qura'n. As the celebrated French writer Henri Troyat said that the older we get, the more we realize that we ac-quired everything from a very early age. In my adult life the tools I re-ceived in my childhood were put to test time and again.

Excursion into an uncharted terrain

In 1963 I came to the United States for postgraduate education and training in surgery. While leaving my family and the city of my birth, I shed a few tears as most young men and women of my background do when they leave the comforting sounds and smells behind. But what surprised me the most was the uneasy feeling and a gnawing sense of loss as I boarded the Alatalia plane in Karachi on my way to the New World. The recurrent doubts as to my ability to cope in an unknown world with all its opportunities, distractions and temptations kept me awake and restless. Somewhere over the Atlantic I penned down my apprehensions in a letter to Dr. Nasir Azam Khan, one of my role models during my medical studies. Dr Khan was not only a brilliant physician and a superb teacher; he was also a practicing Muslim and a pious man. If anyone had an answer to my dilemma, it had to be him, I thought.

A few weeks later when I had settled into my job as an intern in a hospital in Toledo, Ohio, I received his answer. He encouraged me to explore the world around me, take advantage of the opportunities and enjoy my life to the fullest within the parameters prescribed by my faith. In essence what he said was that I would have to get out and ride the fence lines with the help of the tools that have been given to me. In the past 38 years I have been doing just that. It has been a wonderful experience in exploring the world around me as I continue to explore my inner self. In this journey I have kept company with many who on the surface may appear different than me but deep down their quest has been just the same. My life has been enriched by their likes.

We all are part of a larger whole but do not realize it most our lives. For me it came into sharp focus after I came to America. To begin with I was extremely lonely and missed the comforting and soothing symbols of religion and culture in my new surroundings. It was my first Christmas in Toledo when Wray and Robert Barber a wonderful couple that I had befriended asked if I would like to join them for Christmas mass in their Episcopal Church. Reluctantly and with much intimidation I attended the service and had a truly uplifting experience. What I heard and what I felt was quiet different than the brim stone and hell fire sermons I thought most preachers (Muslims as well as Christians) deliver to their congregations. There was beautiful music, uplifting hymns and a message of peace and brotherhood. Many an evening was spent in the Barbars country farm outside Toledo discussing religion, history and myriad other subjects with that wonderful couple.

The lingering smell of burnt flesh

Most religions are, under certain circumstances, capable of showing an ugly and brutal face to the followers of other religions. In the Indian subcontinent there was much amity between Muslims and Hindus but during the struggle for independence from the British the seeds of discord were sown that resulted in much hatred and violence at the time of independence. The partition of the subcontinent in 1947 into Muslim Pakistan and a predominantly Hindu India swept aside the historic amity between the followers of these two religions and in a frenzy of communal bloodletting the extreme Muslims, Hindus and Sikhs let loose a reign of terror on each other. One million people were put to sword and another 4 to 5 million became refugees. This was an unprecedented human tragedy of enormous proportions and it was done in the name of religion.

During that frenzy armed gangs of vigilantes would attack convoys, caravans and trains carrying innocent Muslims, Hindus and Sikhs to the safety of their newly created homelands. Trains would arrive at the destination with not a single living person on board. Some people in my hometown of Peshawar decided to settle the score by killing Hindus and Sikhs.

A number of Hindu families lived in our neighborhood at the end of a narrow alley. The bloodthirsty hoodlums blocked the narrow alley and set fire to their homes. It was surreal even for a nine-year old boy to smell the stench of burning human flesh permeating the air. As the *muezzin* called for prayers from the corner mosque his chant reverberated the neighborhood in the backdrop of the billowing smoke and muffled screams of the trapped people. There was something terrible amiss. The noble human spirit had turned evil, religious teachings were set aside in an orgy of wanton killing of the innocent men, women and children. Even now when I am in Peshawar and hear the call for prayers from the corner mosque I smell the pungent odor seeping out of the deep recesses of my mind.

Most of the Hindus and Sikhs left the city for the safety of India but handfuls stayed back and were given protection by their Muslim neighbors and friends. There is a Hindu temple in the city and whenever I am in Peshawar I visit the place to remember the innocent victims of that ugly incident and remind myself that humanity does extend beyond the confines of one's own faith. In 1947 some believers of my religion turned the sublime into profane and 54 years later I still have a deep gnaw in the pit of my stomach. It is this brutality against mankind by the followers of one's own religion that forces many adherents to denounce religion and leave the fold. In times like these one always falls back on one's own experiences to maintain a perspective and to realize that it is not the religion itself but some of its followers who distort the teachings to justify their action.

Religious arrogance comes in many shapes and shades. On the one extreme is the example I have given above. On the flip side are those who consider themselves the only true believers and therefore feel duty bound to convert others to their own brand of religion.

The arrogance of piety

In my lifetime I have been invited to convert to many religions, including the one I already profess to. Instead of engaging in a fruitless and potentially contentious debate I politely decline their invitation. How could a zealot preach that the rest of the humanity is wrong? How could any body be so arrogant to claim an exclusive connection with God to the exclusion of the rest of us?

A number of years ago I struck up a conversation with a surgeon in one of the hospitals. Actually he approached me and asked me a question about my faith. No sooner had I given him the answer, he started to preach. He told me that true salvation was only through his brand of Christianity and that since I was a good person I should think hard about my salvation. He offered to help me understand the concept of true salvation and that he and his fellow parishioners would be too happy to help me see the light and come onto the right path. I thanked him for interest in my salvation and told him that if I ever feel the need I will call upon him. He did not contact me again. I felt no need to contact him either.

At another time while waiting for my flight at the Islamabad airport in

Pakistan a young Muslim man approached me and started to preach. He was wearing the two-piece white garment of a pilgrim. He belonged to the fast expanding group of Muslim missionaries, the *tablighis*, who are in the habit of preaching to the choir. Most of them are marginally educated young men who having read a few books on religion and having been indoctrinated into proselytizing take up to three months off their work to beat the pavement to convert the already converted. Their motive is two folds: to invite other Muslims to their way of thinking and secondly to earn celestial points, *sawab*, which will help them in the hereafter.

I listened to his preaching with patience but with a bit of resentment. In a celestial pyramid scheme his only interest was to reach the top of the pyramid so he could claim a piece of choice real estate in paradise. After he finished giving me the usual stick and carrot routine, I told him that I was not a Muslim. He was startled. I also told him that I respected his religion tremendously and that I would pray for the acceptance of his offering of pilgrimage. Now it was interesting and a bit amusing to see his discomfort at knowing that I was outside the circle he was familiar with. He did not know how to talk to some one in any other currency but his own. Most likely he had not talked to a non-Muslim before.

He and his ilk roam the countryside in Europe and America to help people understand Islam. They end up talking to only Muslims and even their fellow-Muslims do not embrace them in their mission. But they are contend that more hard ship they endure in the process of spreading the word, more *sawab* or celestial credit they would receive. The young man at the airport having got stuck in his own groove, grappled for words to communicate with a 'non-believer' and having found none left abruptly to rejoin his group.

There is a common thread of selfishness and arrogance of piety in the two examples I mentioned above. Any one who thinks the way to salvation is only through his or her way of thinking is either a fool or a megalomaniac. I have suffered both kinds and partially at the hands of the believers of my own faith. I do not think any one religion or philosophy can claim to be superior to any other. This thought should give pause to over zealous missionaries who with bread in one hand and the holy book in the other prey on the helpless, the hungry and the destitute of the world.

Before embarking upon converting others we need to seek and find the true religion within ourselves. This requires separating the essentials from the cultural add-ons that have over time become part of the religion. It is not an easy process.

An Indian 'heretic'

Moulana Abu Kalam Azad was a political leader in pre-independence India and served as the first education minister of India in the post-independence government of Jawahar Lal Nehru. He was also a great literary figure and a renowned Islamic scholar.

Azad* was born into a hierarchical Muslim family of teachers and scholars. The family traced their lineage to Prophet Muhammad and because of that connection they were accorded great reverence and respect by their disciples and other Muslims. His father ran an exclusive religious school in their home where boys were taught a broad religious education encompassing literature, philosophy, logic as well as Arabic, Persian and Urdu languages. As a young prodigy, Azad finished his formal religious schooling in his early teens and was given an unprecedented responsibility of becoming a teacher in the school. What baffled and confused the young scholar was the rigid interpretation of religion and a total taboo for fine arts. He was interested in music but the customs and religious interpretation did not permit him to pursue that interest. He was also uncomfortable with the way the disciples and followers kissed his father's hands and showed a reverence that bordered on worship. To him this was not in the true spirit of religion. He would, with the help of trusted servants, make clandestine visits to some of the musicians in town to indulge in his passion.

Years later he wrote that in order to make sense he had to demolish the entire edifice of what was given to him as religion and rebuilt his faith on new foundations. By doing that he was able to make sense of not only his

*Because he was on the side of Indian National Congress in demanding a unified India at independence, he was shunned and maligned by those Muslims who wanted a separate homeland for Muslims in the Indian subcontinent. Muhammad Ail Jinnah, the founder of Pakistan, called Azad an errand boy of Gandhi and refused to meet him during negotiations for independence.

own faith but also other religions as well. He did not find it contradictory to enjoy music and to indulge in some of other pleasures that were denied to him by the cultural-religious traditions practiced by his very orthodox family.

In some ways we all undergo some sort of metamorphosis in our beliefs. We learn either by introspection or by stumbling and falling in the traps. Far from being static, religion is a dynamic phenomenon where we continue to rediscover new nuances and in the process keep re-discovering ourselves. But it is not easy and there are difficulties abound. As Maurice Maeterlinck, the Belgian playwright and a Nobel laureate in Literature, said in 1907," at every crossway on the road that leads to the future, (tradition) has placed, against each of us ten thousand men to guard the past".

The devil and the pebbles

In 1982 I went to Mecca for pilgrimage. Our small group of eight people had their roots in India, Syria, Pakistan and Palestine. Though we all professed to the same creed and observed the same rituals, our understanding of those rituals differed.

The Muslim pilgrimage consists of a series of rituals spread over many days and performed in four separate locations in and around Mecca. One of the rituals is to throw pebbles at three stone pillars in a symbolic gesture to renounce devil. According to Muslim traditions it was here outside Mecca that the devil had tried to dissuade Prophet Abraham from sacrificing his son as commanded by the Lord. During this phase of pilgrimage there are tens of thousands of people trying to throw pebbles at the pillars. In great many cases the pebbles do not reach the intended target but end up pelting the heads of the people in front. I decided to forgo the ritual. My companions were adamant that my pilgrimage was not complete for I had deliberately missed an important ritual. On my part I did not care. I was more interested in the safety of people ahead of me than inflicting pain on the proverbial devil. While trying to find an appropriate angle to throw pebbles I had received some of them on the back of my head by over zealous pilgrims. It is the same in everyday life where in the process of practicing our religion, unintentionally we end up hurting those who happen to be in the way.

During the same visit I felt at peace sitting in one corner of the grand mosque contemplating and meditating. You are not supposed to just sit around the sanctuary however. You are supposed to be performing ritualistic supplications and chanting of prayers. Like Moulana Azad, I also felt, in a different context though, that sometimes in strict adherence to rituals we lose the underlying spirit. Ever since that visit to Mecca I have been collecting pebbles but have been throwing them at the demons of self-doubt and uncertainty within me.

It is difficult to explain religion on a rational level. One has to take the rituals and traditions in their spirit and not in their literal form. Prayer, fasting, alms giving and pilgrimage are devices that help connect us to our very inner self and in the process make us better persons. Individually every ritual is important and necessary to help us achieve harmony in life but mere blind adherence to rituals misses the spirit behind them. Some people chase letters while others seek spirit behind the letters. I prefer the later path.

While individually a great number of Muslims follow this concept, such discussions are sorely missing at community and societal level among Muslims. In order to revive the spirit one has to indulge in a healthy and spirited intellectual debate. Amongst Muslims the roots of this intellectual apathy go back a thousand years or more.

The forgotten tool

Islam provides a unique concept for the interpretation of religious law according to the times we live in. It is called *ijtehad* or independent reasoning and was used rather frequently by Sunni scholars in the first few hundreds years of Islamic history. It was mainly due to the exercise of *ijtehad* that different Sunni schools of thought emerged in the Islamic world. There are four main schools of Sunni thought and they are named after their founders. These schools are called Humbli, Shaafi, Maalaki and Hanafi.

Sometime in the beginning of the tenth century it was felt that the above mentioned Sunni schools of law had reached a level of maturity where all possible legal questions had already been addressed and therefore it was not necessary to indulge in the process of *ijtehad*. The scholars were afraid that an ongoing *ijtehad* would invite innovations that could be detrimental to the spirit of religion. From that point on the intellectual curiosity in religious thought gave way to searching for answers in commentaries that had been written in the past. This all but stifled the debate that is so vital for ongoing revival and growth of religion. On the other hand Shia branch of Islam did not abandon *ijtehad* completely and still believes in the process but under strict conditions.

A slide back to the past

During the colonial rule, many reformist movements sprang up in the Muslim and Arab world to protect Muslim identity from what was thought to be the corrupting influences of Western culture. Diverse individuals from different parts of the Muslim world led these movements. In the Arabian Peninsula it was Muhammad Ibn Abd al-Wahhab (1703-1791), in Iran and Afghanistan Jamal ad-Din al-Afghani (1839-1897), in Egypt Muhammad Abduh (1849-1905) and in the Indian subcontinent a number of Muslim scholars in the city of Deoband in the mid 19th century led these efforts. While these revival movements (and many others with the same purpose) differed slightly in their interpretation of Islam, their underlying objective was to revive Islam to its simple and pristine roots that lay in 7th century Arabia. Two of these movements would have profound effects on the politics of the Indian subcontinent and Afghanistan in the coming centuries.

The Wahhabi movement of Arabia was a non-political religious movement that interpreted religion in the light of the Qura'n and Sunnah and rejected all cultural influences on religious practices. The Wahhabis helped Ibn-Saud, the founder of the present day Saudi Arabia, to subdue diverse tribes and forge them into a Saudi nation. In return Ibn Saud agreed to let the Wahhabi clergy enforce their interpretation of Islam in the kingdom. Their interpretation strips the religion of all cultural and ethnic trappings to a simple, spartan and a bit harsh version. In Saudi Arabia criminals are dealt with swiftly and harshly, murderers are beheaded in public, women are required to wear a veil and a vigilant religious police makes sure men attend mosques for obligatory prayers and observe dawn to dusk fasting during the month of Ramadan. So when oil rich Saudi Arabia started helping socio-religious causes and religious institutions in Muslim countries, it also started exporting Wahhabi Islam to those countries. During the war against the Soviet Union, the Afghan Mujahideen received, in addition to petro-dollars, a hefty helping of Wahhabi ideology as well. Osama Bin Laden was the extreme manifestation of the rigid and un-yielding Wahhabi philosophy.

An Indian experiment

In 1857 some native soldiers rebelled against the British rule in India in what came to be known as the Sepoy Mutiny. After the rebellion was ruthlessly crushed, the British unleashed a reign of terror against a cross section of Indian population but particularly against the Muslims. The British blamed Bahadur Shah Zafar, the last of the Muslim Mogul kings for instigating the uprising even though the king had neither the power nor the resources for this purpose. His influence was limited to Delhi's Red Fort where he was a virtual prisoner of the British.

In the demoralizing aftermath of the Mutiny some Muslim clergy came to the conclusion that God had punished them for ignoring the teachings of their religion. In an effort to revive the so-called slumbering Muslim masses, a revival movement sprang up in India to help re-connect Muslims with their spiritual roots.

For this purpose the Muslim scholars and clergy established a school in the city of Deoband in what is present day India. The school curriculum was based on only the religious studies to the exclusion of all other subjects that they thought represented the education of their British masters. The graduates of this school served as preachers and imams. After the success of the school in Deoband tens of such schools sprang up through out India and some in the Far East as well. It is interesting to note that a good number of Afghan boys also studied in these schools and carried back with them the Deobandi philosophy to Afghanistan. In another one and a half-century the Deobandi philosophy would come to fruition in the form of the Taliban of Afghanistan and the rise of militant fundamentalism in Pakistan.

Just about the time that the Deobandi movement was getting a foothold in British India, a progressive educational movement was launched in the country. This movement emphasized the need for modern scientific education in addition to religious instructions. The proponents of this movement realized that it was only through modern education that their youth would be able to compete in a fast changing post industrial-revolution world. Such education was also necessary if muslim youth were to compete for government jobs.

The Deobandis and their likes vehemently opposed this idea and the leader of the forward outlook, Sir Seyyed Ahmad Khan, was labeled an apostate and a heretic. Sir Seyyed was a thoughtful and open-minded religious scholar who did not find any religious constraint in cooperating with the British or accepting their help in the cause of education for his people. With the help of the British he started the Anglo Oriental College in Aligarh that in due course matured into the Aligarh Muslim University and would be a model for such institutions throughout British India. Islamia College, the institution that I attended in Peshawar, had been modeled after the one in Aligarh.

The opposing philosophies that dictated the establishment of these two institutions in India interacted but only as adversaries and for all practical purposes they remained on parallel tracks. While the western educated Muslims would play a pivotal role in shaping public policy in pre-independent India and after 1947 in Pakistan, the Deobandi philosophy would wait a full 145 years before claiming power in Afghanistan in the form of the Taliban.

Why this dichotomy and discord when the principles of religion are rather clear cut and not difficult to understand? Why should the faithful be obliged to choose between two opposing philosophies of education? Is there any historic relevance to this tug of war?

Personal quest to understand religion and its impact on our lives is often swept away by the orthodox/liberal debate. To me the distinction is not that easy or ready-made. In many ways we are both. On the one extreme to the right are those who take every bit of scripture and the traditions of the prophet in a literal sense. They are more ritualistic and can not see the forest for the trees. On the other extreme are the liberals who are Muslims in name only and are totally removed from the practice of religion. In between are the great majority of Muslims who may not be very observant but are nevertheless dedicated to the faith and live it to the best of their ability. The Islamic extreme right, just as certain fringe elements in other religions, has hijacked the religion and considers it as the true custodian of the orthodox religious traditions and therefore the rightful representative of Islam. Unfortunately this kind of self-righteousness rules outs any accommodation with other religions and is prone to create paranoia of others. Just as nationalism can turn into ultra-nationalism and fascism under certain circumstances, religious fundamentalism also has the ability to turn into militancy and occasionally into terrorism. The events of September11, 2001 attest to this.

We are all equal as long as you accept my point of view

In my concept of a community of faith, all believers, irrespective of their outlook and their interpretations, are parts of the community. It is like a circle or the shade of a large tree. Any one who professes to the basic tenets is within the circle and in the shade. Within this circle people might differ with each other in certain practices and interpretations but they are still inside the circle. The extreme right considers itself to be the bull's eye and delegate others with differing views to be in the periphery.

A number of years ago we invited a well-known Islamic scholar to the Islamic Center of Greater Toledo in our Visiting Scholars Program. He talked the talk and walked the walk and was quite impressive in presenting what he thought was the true face of Islam. His comments were general and appeared to be inclusive of all Muslims. Later in a small group discussion I gave him the analogy of the circle of believers and asked him if he considered those Muslims who believe in all the tenets but practice religion in a liberal way to be also in the center of the circle. His answer was startling. To him such people should strive to become good Muslims and thus get close to the center. In his mind there was no question that his brand of religion was the focal point and anyone not subscribing to his way of thinking was in the periphery. He was totally oblivious that there may be many such centers and that compared to some of them he could be in the periphery. Certainly the Taliban of Afghanistan would not consider him a true representative of Islam. And in so many words he was saying the same thing to me.

Such unintentional arrogance is the main impediment to a religious renaissance in the Muslim world. Every one on the spectrum from conservatives to liberals lay claim to the legacy of Prophet Muhammad and considers himself the true inheritor of his traditions. For over 1400 years he has been the focus of reverence and a source of inspiration for all Muslims and for quite a few non-Muslims as well. Who was this man who continues to exert such an enormous influence in the lives of Muslims?

A man for all seasons

Born an orphan in 570 AD in Mecca, Muhammad was a contemplative young man in his youth. He worked as a shepherd boy and later took business trips to Syria on behalf of a rich businesswoman of Mecca. Whenever he could, he would retire to a mountain cave outside Mecca for meditation. He was forty years old when Archangel Gabriel brought the divine message to him in that cave. For the next twenty-three years he received revelations, sometimes spontaneously and sometimes in response to his prayers for guidance for a particular issue or a problem. The Qura'n is the compilation of all those revelations and we Muslims consider it the true word of God as revealed to Muhammad.

As it is with any new religion, the citizens of Mecca did not take kindly to his preaching a religion that contradicted their pagan beliefs and challenged their tribal traditions. As his message started to spread in Mecca so did the level of opposition and persecution of Muhammad and the handful of his followers. After a few years of preaching in Mecca he left for the northern city of Medina where he established the first community of the faithful and laid the political and ideological foundations of a city-state. His migration or *hijra* to Medina is considered a watershed event in the history of Islam and its importance is underlined by the fact that Islamic calendar takes its start from *hijra* and not from Prophet's birth date or from the time of his prophecy. Eventually Muhammad was able to win over the tribes and by the time he died in 632 AD at age 63, the entire Arabian Peninsula had converted to his new religion.

Muhammad was born in a society where personal gains and individual honor took precedent over societal responsibilities. It is remarkable that as a contemplative young man he kept himself away from all the vices that were norm in the society. Drunken brawls, sexual promiscuousity and gambling were considered virtues. People killed at the slightest provocation and the practice of female infanticide was a common practice. Through all this Muhammad remained a pious and trustworthy man that earned him the nickname of *Al-amin* or the trustworthy one. He was illiterate but preached the virtues of knowledge. As head of the community of the faithful in Medina he laid the foundation of a state that was fare, compassionate and accountable to people. And all through this he never claimed to be anything but an ordinary man who was chosen by God to spread His message. In the brief span of 23 years he transformed a feudal and tribal society of ancient Arabian Peninsula into a cohesive classless society. In so doing he changed the course of history and in turn changed the world.

Here are some of his recorded sayings:

The first thing created by God was the intellect.
The most excellent jihad is the one for the conquest of self.
The ink of the scholar's pen is more sacred than the blood of the martyr.
One learned man is harder on the devil than a thousand ignorant worshipers.
Riches are not from an abundance of worldly goods but from a contended mind.

He who wishes to enter paradise must please his mother and
father.

No man is a true believer unless he desires for his brother that
which he desires for himself.

When the bier of any one passes by you, whether Jew,
Christian or Muslim, rise to your feet (in respect).

The thing that is lawful but disliked by God is divorce.

Heaven lies at the feet of your mothers.

Women are the twin halves of men.

Actions will be judged according to intentions.

The proof of a Muslim's sincerity is that he pays no attention
to what is not his business.

That person is nearest to God who instead of taking revenge,
forgives.

Assist any person oppressed, whether Muslim or non-Muslim.

Modesty and chastity are parts of faith.

Muhammad's impact and influence on the life of Muslims is as vivid and strong today as it was during his lifetime. His life and his deeds remain the source of inspiration where the faithful try to emulate him in their lives. Some follow his example by physically molding their lives the way the prophet lived. Others look for the meaning behind the acts and try to follow him in spirit. Occasionally these two approaches collide across the orthodox and liberal divide. This needs some elaboration.

The fountainhead of religion

Qura'n is the cornerstone of Islam and is the source of everything Islamic. It is a book of guidance, prayer, laws, and stories. Some of the passages in the Qura'n are explicit and clear whereas other passages are allegorical and mystic. During his life the prophet, when asked by his disciples, would elaborate on some of the revelations. Those explanations and his other sayings and quotations are not part of the Qura'n but are compiled separately in a body of works called the *Hadith*. The *Hadith* literature also contains narratives about prophet's personality, demeanor and his conduct.

For some Muslims, particularly the progressive ones, some of the Hadith pose a problem. Some of the Hadith were collected and recorded decades after the death of the prophet in a second or third hand account. Some of the Hadith are contradictory to the scripture and still some others negate some of prophet's teachings. The majority of Muslims however accept only those Hadith which are consistent with the message of the Quran and the teachings of the prophet. But some Muslims, particularly those with orthodox or fundamentalist bend, do not reject any Hadith, as long as these are part of the six main collections that were compiled in the 9th century. Two of these collections, *Sahih Bukhari* and *Sahih Muslim* are considered more authentic. Unfortunately even in these so-called authentic collections there are many Hadith that contradict the Qura'n and are contrary to the spirit of religion. It is quite possible that people who wanted to legitimize their own thoughts in the name of the prophet fabricated many of these sayings at a later date. To avoid this trap a number of Muslims reject the *Hadith* all together and rely only on the *Qura'n* for guidance. But the majority of Muslims accept only those *Hadith* that are consistent with the overall message of the religion. The battle between the orthodoxy and moderation is in essence dictated by how one looks at the *Hadith*.

There may be disagreement on the authenticity of some of Prophet's sayings but there is no disagreement about his life and his deeds. As it has been mentioned earlier for a great majority of Muslims, the prophet remains the ultimate human perfection and in their daily lives they strive to live up to that ideal. Some Muslims of orthodox persuasion pay a lot more emphasis on the way he talked, dressed, ate and interacted with other people. Hence their emulation of keeping a beard, wearing long robes, speaking gently, eating simply, using a tree twig to clean their teeth and living a simple life. Others, more liberals, do not pay much attention to how he looked but what he said and taught. They connect to him through his deeds and his conduct. The former are more ritualistic and accepts older interpretations and commentaries as final; the later want to understand the scripture according to times. Both of these groups and hundreds of shades thereof strive for the legitimacy of their rightful central place within the community of believers.

Amidst this entire debate, albeit a contentious one, I always think of one person who was above the foray and practiced religion in an unassuming and gentle way. She understood the spirit of Islam better than the zealot mullahs, the all-knowing liberals or the academic scholars. It was my mother.

An illiterate scholar

My mother was an illiterate woman who except for her ability to read the Qura'n in Arabic, a foreign language for her, could not read or write. She learned to read the book as a young girl but never knew the meaning of it. She carried the tradition and went on to pass that gift to three generations. Along with other women of the household she lived a secluded life within the four walls of her home. If there were an occasion to venture outside of the home for a wedding or a death in the family, she would, as was the custom, cover herself with an all-encompassing garment called *burqa*. In those days, in the twenties and thirties, she had no access to newspapers, magazines or radio. Radio came in the fifties and the television much later in the seventies. Even from that secluded and confining world she was able to touch the lives of her children, her neighbors and all those who came in contact with her. She imparted on them an abiding belief in the nobility of human spirit and also in the goodness of her own beliefs. She lived her religion with comfort, compassion and with humor. Even when she interacted with people of different faiths, in this case the Christian women-sweepers that came to clean and to visit, she accepted them for what they were. She always saw goodness in others even if they happen to be on the opposite side of a religious divide.

At the time in the old walled city of Peshawar, as is even now in some parts of the city, houses lacked modern sanitary facilities. We had running water from a spigot but no flush toilets. There were two outhouses on the terrace on the top floor. Every day a Christian woman sweeper would come with her basket, clean the outhouses and haul the refuse to a nearby dump. The men and women who cleaned toilets and hauled refuse were considered a notch below the others and were treated accordingly. My mother, to the chagrin and discomfort of others in the family, would have these women sit on the floor by her and visit. She would save leftover food for them and was not hesitant to fix them a cup of tea. In contrast, others members of the family, in total disregard for the teachings of their religion- equality, compassion and acceptance- were quiet comfortable with this selective apartheid. If we were ever rude to our domestic help or the sweepers, she would give us a proper dressing down. They are all children of the same God, she would say on those occasions.

A lowly sweeper and a status conscious surgeon

Apparently I had not paid much attention to that oft-repeated refrain of hers. After returning from America in 1970, I took a job at my alma mater Khyber Medical College and worked as a surgeon in the teaching hospital. On this one particularly busy and hectic day, when I was in the midst of seeing patients in the crowded out patient clinic, a man barged in without an appointment and without consideration to the hundreds of others waiting their turn. Before I could scold him for his rude intrusion and have him thrown out, he said 'Doctor *Sahib*, I went to see the elder *Bibi* to seek her advice for a sick relative and she told me to bring the patient to you'. Since the man had invoked my mother's name, I saw the patient, did what ever needed to be done but I was annoyed and irritated. That evening I brought up the subject and told my mother how the sweeper from our old neighborhood had so rudely interrupted my work and embarrassed me in front of my staff.

The lady, much wiser than her years, listened to me while her characteristic beautiful smiled played on her lips. When I finished complaining, she gently reminded me that I had become a surgeon because of the sacrifices of those little people who had made it possible for me to receive a free education. If I were not going to look after their interests, who would? Therefore I should not think too big of myself.

In her book the deprived, the disfranchised and the down trodden had the right to jump fences and crash lines because that was the only way they could be heard or noticed. It was amazing that considering her rigid hierarchical background she would identify with the poor and was willing to go against the tide to support them. This to me was the ideal Islamic way even though she never went to a school to learn it. She knew the right from the wrong.

The dichotomy of belief in the equality of man and the practice of apartheid towards a segment of the society has always been in the back of my mind. My upbringing in a mostly monolithic culture did not prepare me for the challenges I would later face in the West. But some how the simple, all- inclusive refrain 'we are all children of the same God' has helped me understand those who look and think differently or profess to a different religion.

In Peshawar religious minorities lived harmoniously with each other. There had never been any incidents of religiously driven crimes against the followers of other religions. At the time of partition of Indian subcontinent into a mostly Muslim Pakistan and a predominantly Hindu India most Hindus and Sikhs left for India leaving behind a small Christian minority. The majority of Muslims have no social interaction with them. Except at work these two communities do not interact socially or visit each other's places of worship. Before coming to the United States in 1963 I had not set foot in a church, a Hindu temple or a Sikh gurdwara even though there were plenty of them in Peshawar.

A Hindu roommate

My roommates during my internship in 1963 were two physicians from India, one Hindu and the other a Christian. The first few months were difficult and awkward for me. I did not care for the traditional anti-Pakistani stance of their native country. In the begging I tried to avoid them but it was not possible living in a small apartment. As time passed I was struck by their warmth, their friendliness and their lack of any obvious prejudice towards me. In time my subtle prejudice towards them was washed away by their attitude towards me and by the echoes of my mother's refrain. Without really trying to win over each other, we became good friends.

Surendra Kumar Bansal , my Hindu roommate, came from a wealthy family from the city of Ambala in Indian Punjab. In due course our families in Pakistan and India got to know the two of us as well. Surendra's father would write to him in Urdu, a language that the son was not very proficient in, so I would act as a translator. His father, after learning of my interest in Urdu literature, would send me literary works of Urdu language

After my internship I stayed in Toledo to study surgery and he headed for Pennsylvania to train in radiology and we lost touch with each other. In 1965 India and Pakistan fought a war over the disputed Himalayan State of Kashmir. When I heard that Pakistani air force had bombarded the city of Ambala in Indian Punjab I was concerned about his family. I wrote him a letter wondering if his family was safe and asked that he convey my concerns and best wished to them in India.

Just about the same time the Indian airforce attacked my hometown of Peshawar. A few days later I received a letter from Surendra expressing the same sentiments that I had expressed in my letter. We both had spontaneously felt for each other's families and our letters bearing those messages had crossed in the mail. The irony of the situation was that perhaps our mutual families in India and Pakistan were cheering the attacks on each other's countries. Somehow we had developed a bond that transcended religious and national boundaries.

A slippery slope

To develop a bond that transcends those boundaries is rather difficult and I have not always been successful in my efforts. National pride does force us, under certain circumstances, to re-pledge our allegiance to the blind gods of pseudo-nationalism. Just as nationalism can lead to ultra-nationalism and that in turn can lead to fascism, we have seen the same rightward slide in some fringe elements of Islam. The devastating attacks on America on September 11, 2001 had its roots in religious fundamentalism where a perceived or real grievance against the US led some of them to turn militants and in turn terrorists. Nazi Germany, post-Soviet Union Yugoslavia and Osama bin Laden are just a few examples of how an ideology, nationalist or religious, can turn ugly, intolerant and violent.

Religion can and has played an important role in building of understanding and acceptance between the followers of various faiths. It falls on the shoulders of the religious leaders to help their followers to achieve that. Unfortunately it has been an exception rather than a rule.

The common thread

There is an inherent built-in suspicion between various religions by virtue of their differing doctrine and theology. But surprisingly there are also many common elements that are more specific than the generalities of charity, goodness and piety. To begin with the three monotheistic religions, Judaism, Christianity and Islam, trace their origins to Patriarch Abraham. All of them believe in oneness of God and all of them share the concept of hereafter and reward and punishment. And all of them stress that salvation can be achieved by sincerely practicing one's faith. If the purpose of religion is to help us excel in our personal and public lives then it does not matter if we use different methods or different routes to achieve that goal. To assert that only one faith has the answer to life's mysteries is to negate the grand design of God for his creation. A compassionate God is common to us all and I do not think that God will banish us to hell fire (or to some celestial wilderness) if we continue to be true to our mutual faiths.

Islam emphasizes prayer, fasting, alms and pilgrimage as essential elements for the development of a devout Muslim. But the underlying running theme in the *Qura'n* is to help the believers in becoming better persons who are good to themselves, their family, their community and to mankind. The rituals in themselves are not the end point but they are the means to reach the end point of achieving goodness. Some people would translate the end point into ultimate salvation. I have no doubt that practicing one's religion faithfully and by trying to become a better person is a reward in itself. The *Qura'n* repeatedly emphasizes that the believers must be good and kind to others and this include all people irregardless of their faith. It does not ask Muslims to be good only to other Muslims. Therefore I am at a loss to see the traditional emphasis by Muslim clergy on *ibadaat-*

the rituals and practices and ignore the concept of *muamalaat*- the worldly affairs or relationships. Both are stressed in the *Qura'n*; they are inter-twined and are important.

All religions need learned leaders to help preserve the teachings of their faith and to pass them on to the next generation. However in the pro-cess of doing that they end up preaching the exclusivity and superiority of their faith. Some how such a sense of superiority, instead of creating har-monious relations, end up pitting one religion against the other. Our priests, pastors, rabbis, imams, pundits and garanthis say the right things when they get together in interfaith meetings. While emphasizing coexistence and respect they embrace each other with open arms. But some of the same clergy when back in their churches, synagogues, mosques, temples and gurdwaras preach the superiority of their faith.

How could we be equal and superior at the same time?

What we need is religious leaders who could look beyond the narrow interpretations of their own religions and develop an open approach to other faiths. Instead of uttering the mantra of tolerance they should talk about acceptance because in religious context tolerance is a negative term. This approach will not diminish our respective faiths but would enhance them.

A new reawakening?

Many Muslims believe that their faith is undergoing a renaissance and that this renaissance is happening in the West. While I agree that a reli-gious renaissance can only happen in a secular democratic society where one is free to express views that are contrary to the conventional wisdom, I have difficulty accepting that we are ready to engage in such a debate about our religion. A renaissance takes into consideration a return of youthful vigor, freshness, zest and productivity. One can not expect such revival from those who are the products of old archaic systems where to question is to commit a sin. It requires the intellectual debate among Muslims in an academic-community setting where old interpretations could be challenged, debated and new ground broken in religious thought and in religious inter-pretations. The Muslims have not taken the lead to indulge in such an exercise. The orthodox thinking which under certain conditions can turn into militancy has cast a long shadow on such efforts. In theocratic Islamic countries to break new ground in religious thought is to literally dig one's grave.

Knowledge and pursuit of knowledge is a recurrent theme in the Qura'n. Prophet Muhammad, illiterate himself, paid much emphasis to learning. He said that it was incumbent upon the believers to pursue knowledge even if they had to travel to China- the farthest point in his days - in that pursuit. And he also said that a scholar's ink is more sacred than the blood of a martyr. Somehow we have a lopsided reversal of the famous saying. The blood of martyrs is very much in the news but the inkwells of the scholars have run dry. They are relying mostly on the works of the scholars of yore. When I think of the lack of original inquiry by Muslim scholars, I am reminded of Washington Irving's essay 'The Art of Bookmaking'. In a hilarious dream scene contemporary scholars dress themselves with cloths stripped off the bodies of ancient writers.

For Muslims to have a continued interest in their religion and to keep the interest of the next generation, they will have to alter their thinking drastically. We need not invent a new face; we need only to brush off the dust that has been accumulating on the true face of religion for centuries. It can be done for it had been done before. It is time for the reconstruction of a new paradigm. That would be the Islamic Reformation.

My journey through life as a Muslim has been exciting and fascinating if at times frustrating. As I get closer to the end of the trail in the midafternoon of my life, I look back at the distance traveled with much satisfaction and also with some pride.

It has been a wonderfully joyous journey.

It still is.

13

BYZANTINE EMPIRE

&

ORTHODOX CHURCH

My Greek son-in-law comes to attention whenever he hears the word Byzantine. Although I have encountered Byzantine architecture in various places during my travels in Europe and Asia, I never knew what the name meant or how it fitted into the history of his Greek religion. The first part of the answer came easy. Istanbul, the beautiful and strategically important city at the Bosporus, was formerly named Constantinople, and before that it was named Byzantium. In AD 395 it became the capital of the Eastern Roman Empire, which is commonly called the Byzantine Empire.

That started me on my quest. Before proceeding further we need to do some backtracking.

Early Christians in Rome were persecuted and remained underground for a couple centuries. After the Roman leader Constantine was converted to Christianity, their lot improved. The Nicene Creed was agreed to at the first ecumenical council of the Christian world, which was held at Nicea in AD 325, and it established the definition of Christian teaching. A generation later, the Holy Roman Empire was separated into its eastern and western halves during an era of economic and political decay in the west. The ecclesiastical authority was divided among various regional high-bishops or patriarchs. The Bishop of Rome was generally recognized as first among these church leaders. The western half of the empire soon became fragmented with barbarian invasions from many directions. As the dark ages descended, the Christian church became scattered among many congregations, but they found ways to continue to communicate. Documents of various kinds, including gospels and apostolic epistles, circulated widely.

Christendom retained at least the formal tradition of unity until 1054, when the Latin-speaking Western church and the Greek-speaking Orthodox Church severed themselves from one another, ostensibly upon the question of adding a word to the Nicene Creed. The older version declared that the "Holy Ghost proceeded from the Father". The Latins wanted to add, and they did add "Filioque", or "from the Son". The Orthodox Church did not agree with this change in theology and would not accept it, because they did not recognize the supremacy of the Bishop of Rome in such matters. Then in effect, the Bishop of Rome and the Patriarch of Constantinople excommunicated each other.

With the final fall of the Western Empire, the Bishop of Rome took over the ancient title of "Pontifex Maximus" which the emperors had held, and so became the supreme priest of the Western tradition. The rift of 1054 ended his influence with the East.

Through several preceding centuries the Eastern Empire had gradually splintered into separate domains which included Egypt, Syria, and Persia. The Muslims had conquered much of the eastern Mediterranean, so the Byzantine Empire was left with only the Balkans, Greece, Sicily, and scattered portions of Italy. Byzantine architecture developed throughout Asia and Europe during the era of their dominance. An example is the Basilica of St. Marks in Venice. This church is one of the major edifices of Catholic Christendom. It was begun in AD 830. Then in the eleventh century after the rift in the church, when the Byzantine controlled this part of Italy, St. Marks was reconstructed into the Byzantine style.

In AD 1025, the Russians accepted Christianity and ecclesiastical rule from Constantinople, which paved the way for the penetration of Byzantine influence in Russia. The Russian church gradually became the dominant factor in the Eastern Orthodox Church. Everyone has seen pictures of the Kremlin in Moscow with the beautiful Byzantine church spires in the background.

In 1071, the Muslim Turks annihilated most of the Byzantine army, and the empire was essentially ended. The decades to follow saw the menace from the Muslim Turks of the east, and plunder from the Crusaders from the west. It was a turbulent and brutal era of history.

At last we come to Greece, my son-in-law, and the Greek Orthodox Church. Through all of the above history, the Christian church within Greece remained under the Patriarch of Constantinople, and later on the Turks. The Greek Orthodox Church did not gain its autonomy until the Greek wars of Independence in the nineteenth century. Since then a close church-state relationship in Greece has existed, which not infrequently resulted in the dominance of the church by the state, and this was particularly true during the two world's wars. The Archbishop of the Greek Church, who is the religious patriarch, resides in Athens. The ritual is very similar to the Roman Catholic Mass, and I feel "at home" when I accompany George and participate in their communion. Greek is the founding language of the Christian religion and of the New Testament; perhaps the Greek Orthodox Church ritual is the most original of the Christian churches.

The rift between the Eastern and Western Catholic church that occurred in 1054 AD is now on the mend. In 1995, Pope John Paul ll. shared the altar with the leader of the Orthodox Church and issued a passionate appeal for unity among the faiths after nearly a millennium apart.

"We cannot remain separate," the pontiff said during a Mass in St. Peter's Basilica. Ecumenical Patriarch Bartholomew joined the pope on the altar above the tomb of S. Peter. The Mass was the highlight of the patriarch's four-day visit to promote reconciliation between the Orthodox and Roman Catholic churches. Who knows if this will lead on to a historic reconciliation among two of the major religions of the world.

14
THE PROTESTANT REFORMATION

My mother was raised a Methodist, but acquiesced to my father's Catholic religion at the time of marriage. It was not a big thing in the frontier towns of western Dakota, where church services were sporadic and sometimes non-existent. We were taught from the Baltimore catechism, but those Sundays when the Catholic missionary was not passing through the territory, we children attended the Methodist Sunday school and learned the King James Bible; as a consequence of being half-Catholic and half-Protestant, I straddled the fence lines between these religions. That was not always easy. There has been great acrimony between the Catholic and Protestant churches through most of my lifetime, indeed, through the last half millennium.

The Protestant Reformation was a major revolt within the Christian Church. Dozens of Protestant religions grew out of the Reformation to stand in direct opposition to the Catholic Church for the past five hundred years. This split reached down into virtually every community in America, and affected not only religious faith, but also the social structures. It often determined where one went to school, what was taught, who one socialized with, who one married and under what conditions. Marriages that mixed two religions often faced conflict. These religious-social circumstances have had a major impact during my life.

This religious revolt did not erupt over night, but built up over a period of several centuries during which controversy dogged the Christian Church. In the thirteenth century there were violent public controversies between Pope Gregory lX and Emperor Frederick, which was to be a forerunner of things to come. During the fourteenth century, the exodus of the Popes to Avignon (in France), and the divisions and disorders of the papacy further stimulated the challenge to Church authority. An English priest, Wycliffe, translated the Bible into English and in the process challenged some of the doctrines of the Mass; particularly the teaching that the bread eaten in the ceremony becomes the actual body of Christ. His writings received wide appeal among laymen throughout parts of Europe. He was denounced by the papacy, and after death his bones were burnt. In Bohemia a few years later, a learned Czech, John Huss, delivered a series of lectures that supported the teachings of Wycliffe, and as a result he was excommunicated. Huss was then decoyed to Constance under a promise of safe conduct by church officials, but once there he was put on trial for heresy. He was ordered to recant his teachings concerning the Mass, particularly his challenge that the consecrated bread does not become in some supernatural way the actual body of Christ. He replied that he could not recant until he was convinced of his error. In AD 1415, in spite of the safe conduct he had been promised, he was burnt alive by church authorities. A colleague of his, Jerome of Prague, under the same circumstances was burnt alive by church authorities in the following year. These outrages were followed by an insurrection of Hussites (followers of Huss) in Bohemia, the first of a series of religious wars that marked the breaking-up of Christendom.

Superimposed on this religious struggle that was brewing during the fourteenth century was the pallor that the Black Death (bubonic plague - spread by fleas on rats) cast over society. This most lethal disaster in known history seemingly came out of no where, and killed perhaps a majority of the population of Europe. It is difficult to comprehend such a catastrophe. The social effects of such an overwhelming disaster proved elusive to pin down, but no doubt had some impact on the religious turmoil.

The reputation of the church sank lower in the fifteenth century during the regimes of mundane popes and prelates and of a clergy that was not always above corruption. The economic exploitation of the people by the Roman Curia for a long time had been one of the grievances denounced by most nations, but this had borne no results. Mediaeval theology had fallen into disrepute, and a new secularist's attitude that was critical toward religion challenged the whole mediaeval world of ideas and beliefs.

Early in the sixteenth century, the church undertook the unusually cynical practice of selling indulgences that mitigated the time in purgatory to raise money for the completion of St. Peter's basilica at Rome. In 1517, a priest named Martin Luther, who was a professor of theology at the University of Wittenberg; visited Rome on the business of his religious order was shocked by the levity and worldly splendor of the papacy and this selling of indulgences. Returning home, he posted on the door of the castle church ninety-five theses, which he undertook to defend against all comers in a public debate.

At first Luther carried on the debate in Latin, but presently took to German, and quickly had the people in ferment. He was ordered by Pope Leo X to recant his views, but refused and fled into hiding, safe under the protection of the Elector of Saxony. Soon there arose a widespread peasant revolt throughout Germany, and the Reformation became full-blown.

During this sixteenth century, the continent exploded into a series of religious revolts led by Luther in Germany, Zwingli in Switzerland, Calvin in France, and Knox in Scotland. "On every front the Catholic Church tried to stem the sweep of Protestantism, but to little avail. All of Scandinavia, England, Scotland, Northern Germany, and Holland were lost. The revolt spread to France."

In 1618 the Thirty Years War was begun, which was to be a showdown between Catholician and Protestantian. "The northern half of Europe became Protestant and industrial; the southern half remained Catholic and agricultural." The conclusion of this was in 1648 with the Treaty of Westphalia, which saw a truce line drawn through the center of Europe.

The acrimony and religious debate between Catholic and Protestants, and even among the various Protestant religious disciplines, continued to rage through the centuries to the present time. In recent years there is a gradual softening of attitudes. Some Catholic historians have now come to look upon the Protestant Reformation with less resentment than their predecessors, and with more sympathetic appreciation of the spiritual and moral function that it has played in history.

Most recently in 1995, Pope John Paul ll. has commented on the division within the Christian Church:

"It is impossible to imagine that this Church, instituted by Christ on the foundation of the apostles and of Peter, should not be one. But we can also understand how over the centuries contact with different political and cultural climates could have led believers to interpret Christ's message with varying emphases.

"Nevertheless, these different approaches to understanding and living out one's faith in Christ can, in certain cases, be complementary; they do not have to be mutually exclusive. Good will is needed in order to realize how various interpretations and ways of practicing the faith can come together and complement each other. There is also the need to determine where genuine divisions start, the point beyond which the faith is compromised. It is legitimate to affirm that the gap between the Catholic and the Orthodox Church is not very wide. On the other hand, with regard to the Churches and the communities originating in the reformation, we must recognize that the gap is considerable wider, since several fundamental elements established by Christ were not respected."

When does the Pope believe that unity will happen?

It is not easy to predict..... The Church was undivided during

**the first millennium; the second was marked by many pro-
found divisions to the East and West, which today need to be
mended.**

He hints that we can look to the third millennium with optimism.   Later
in 1995, nearly six hundred years after Huss was burned alive at the stake
by Church officials in Bohemia, now the Czech Republic, the Pope visited
the same area and asked the world's forgiveness with the following comments:

**"Today I, the Pope of the Church of Rome, in the name of all
Catholics, ask forgiveness for the wrongs inflicted on non-
Catholics during the turbulent history of these peoples."**

A Vatican Spokesman commented, "He is pushing hard on the accel-
erator toward unity. The main obstacle is not doctrine but history with all
its prejudices."

Five years later in March of 2000, in a landmark public confession,
Pope John Paul II begged God's forgiveness for sins committed or con-
doned by Roman Catholics over the past 2,000 years, including sexism,
racism, hatred of Jews and violence in the defense of the Catholic faith. It
was truly a historic moment as the pope listed or eluded to a wide range of
victims of Catholic hostility, prejudice and indifference as he asked his
church to enter its third millennium with a purified conscience. These
victims included heretics, Protestants, Jews and other non-Christians, immigrants, ethnic minorities, women, abused children and the unborn.

"We forgive and ask forgiveness", the Pope said several times during
his Solemn Day of Pardon Mass in St. Peter's Basilica, a crowning moment
of the papacy that has made repentance a central theme. While he de-
fended the church as,

**"A wonderful wealth of holiness, of missionary ardor, of total dedi-
cation to Christ and to our neighbor,"** but also acknowledged that, **"some
of our brothers have been unfaithful to the Gospel"**. Their failings, he

said, were especially glaring in the second millennium- a period covering the holy wars of the Crusades, the executions of heretics and other non-Catholics by courts of the Inquisition, and the forced conversions of native peoples in Africa and the Americas.

Without specifying those bloody chapters, Pope John Paul added:

> **"We ask forgiveness for the divisions among Christians, for the use of violence that some Christians have committed in the service of the truth and for the attitudes of mistrust and hostility sometimes assumed toward followers of other religions."**

The Pope certainly set the stage during the Jubilee Year for a greater ecumenical spirit among peoples of all religious faiths.

About 85% of the people of the world adhere to some religion. Here are the current statistics.

Religions	**Population%**	**Adherents**	**% Annual Gwt.**
Christian	32.54%	1,973 billion	+1.43%
Muslim	21.09	1,279	+2.17
Non-religious	15.46	938	+0.97
Hindu	13.52	820	+1.44
Buddhist	6.60	400	+1.21
Chinese	6.31	383	-1.28
Traditional ethnic	2.90	176	+1.72
Sikh	0.34	20.5	+1.70
Jewish	0.24	14.2	+0.63
Other	1.00	60.8	+1.53
Total	100.00%	6,065.1 billion	+1.39%

Johnstone and Mandryk, *Operation World*, Paternoster Lifestyles, UK, 2001, Pg. 2

I am not sure how much of the third millennium I will see, but I question that I will be around to witness a scene with the Roman Catholic, Orthodox, and Protestant Christian Churches, plus Jews and Muslims, celebrating Mass and sharing the same communion together in the basilica of St.

Peters. There are too many historical prejudices and cultural differences in the halls of the Vatican, Protestant headquarters, Istanbul, Jerusalem, and Mecca to permit this. Despite this, I do anticipate that Christians, Jews, and Muslims down in the trenches at the grass root level, who are more interested in the simple teachings of Christ, Moses, Muhammad, and the other prophets than in advanced theology or dogma, will gradually come together in a common communion. This ecumenical spirit has already been started in my life. The cowboy, Pope John Paul II, is vigorously riding the fence lines, trying to make peace between the cattle ranchers and the sheep men.

15

EVANGELICAL CHRISTIAN

"Evangelical: Christian churches that emphasize the teachings and authority of the Scriptures, especially of the New Testament, in opposition to the institutional authority of the church itself, and that stress as paramount the tenet that salvation is achieved by personal conversion to faith in the atonement of Christ."

Most of us have surfed through TV channels and found an Evangelist religious service like one conducted by the Reverend Billy Graham in a football stadium, or the Reverend Schuller in the beautiful Crystal Cathedral in Anaheim, California. The service we witness typically consists of reading scripture from the Bible interspersed with music, then preaching in which the scripture is related to some aspect of our lives. Then the minister will invite those present to "receive Christ". People walk forward in a solemn manner as their spiritual commitment to Christ. We often become caught-up emotionally in the service, and make the same spiritual commitment as we sit with our TV. Millions of people engage in this form of worship, and that includes me. Those who choose to worship in this manner are often called a "Born Again Christian".

This Evangelist service has become a modern religious phenomenon, but its roots go back to the time of the earliest Protestant movement. While we do not think of Martin Luther as Evangelical, he first used the expression, "born again". During the time he was a monk in the Catholic Church, Luther had despaired of pleasing a God because of all the hurdles imposed by the church. Although he lived a blameless life, he felt he was a sinner with an uneasy conscience before God. He never felt he had pleased God with his works, nor was contrite enough, nor his confessions adequate.

Luther then formulated his "Doctrine of Justification". Man could not save himself. God provides everything necessary for "justification", the restoration of a relationship between the sinner and God. We are able to observe the precepts of religion simply because God has saved us. For Luther, this revelation, "Made me feel as though I had been born again, and as though I had entered through open gates into paradise itself". He came to believe that assurance of salvation was to be found by divine grace through faith, which he thought the Catholic theology had obscured by giving equal weight to the efficacy of good works.

Christians are "born again" to a new faith in God, and a rejection of the intermediaries that stand between them and the Divine. The obstacles include much of the structure and doctrines of the traditional church. For example, an Evangelist "will reject what they see as the cult of the saints," and would not think of asking some one designated as a saint to intercede between themselves and their God.

The experience of being "born again" was crucial. It was absolutely necessary to experience "God continually breathing, as it were, upon the human soul ... filling the Christian with a continual, thankful love to God that was consciously felt .... And which made it natural and, in a manner, necessary, to love every child of God with kindness, gentleness and long suffering." One has this experience when one "receives Christ". Doctrines about God were useless and could be damaging. "Academics could go on 'chattering about the mystery of the Trinity', but the meaning of the doctrine was not the relations of the three Persons to one another but 'what they are to us'".

Down through the centuries the Protestant movement took different forms as churches were formed with differing theologies and many of these would not be called "Evangelical" in the modern use of the term. During the 20th century, the Evangelical label began to be applied to the interdenominational efforts at outreach. Revivalism was typified by "revival meetings" and the itinerant ministries. Their outstanding 20th century successor is Billy Graham, the leading figure in U.S. Evangelicalism since World War Two.

The Evangelical religious experience with its less structured, less doctrinaire, simpler form of worship seems to have an appeal to many people who have rejected their prior structured religion and opt for something without complex dogma, or those who believe in God but never had exposure to any formal religion, and a particular appeal to people who feel lost in the depths of despair who seek a simple faith they can cling to.

One of my high school classmates and a life-long friend is Dr. Wilbur Wacker, pastor of the Calvary Church of the Coastlands. When I am in Southern California, I attend the Evangelical Sunday services with Dr. Wacker's congregation. It is a moving experience. He now has silver hair and looks quite distinguished, and indeed he is distinguished with a lifetime of accomplishments: Oxford University, U.S. Military War College, delegate to many Billy Graham Convocations, and throughout his ministries he traveled to over 50 nations on four continents preaching and teaching. He had a beautiful singing voice in our high school men's quartet, but now relies on a marvelous choir that performs, interspersed with reading of scripture. Then he preaches, and his messages hit the nail on the head. He was raised, like me, in the frontier environment of western South Dakota during the depression era of the 1930's, and no up-bringing could be more appropriate to someone who aspires to be "born again".

Evangelist ministers sing, pray, worship, and preach, but are not given to writing of treatises or dogma. Out of respect for their worship, I will leave it at that.

16
RIDING THE FENCES

By The Rev. Joel P. Miller

Pastor, St. Francis of Assisi Episcopal Church

In my circles asking an Anglican priest who he is and what fences he has ridden along in life could be a best seller. Episcopalians tend to regard themselves as special, an exclusive and perhaps a self-absorbed lot who enjoy to a fault their own stories and histories. For others I fear that such a chronicle may sound overly indulgent. Historically the Episcopal Church has presented itself as a unique purveyor of truth within Christendom. We consider ourselves special and have been an enigma for both Protestant and Catholic Christians. Currently we are perhaps best known for the disagreements and controversies that our bishops engage in.

The Apostle Peter wrote in his epistle 1900 years ago that the church is a "peculiar people." Often I have mused that Peter envisaged that strain of Christianity that was to emerge from England some three hundred years after his death when he coined those words: a peculiar people. We are a unique people and have had a unique history. St. Alban, the first martyr in the British Isles, and his Celtic successors etched their own perspective of the faith onto the tableau of Church long before Christianity ever officially arrived in the British Isles. As an Episcopal priest I feel that this history is not only part of my legacy it has fashioned my own spiritual DNA. Allow me to give a brief history of the Church of England and its 18th century descendent: The Episcopal Church before I tell my own story.

For over 1400 years the Church of England has made a religion out of riding the fences. Finding the middle course midst controversy is the stuff of which we are made. From our origins in the British Isles, Roman and Celtic Christians were constrained to look for common boundaries where they could meet and commune. Anglican history has proven over again that religion as well as politics makes for strange bedfellows and awkward relationships. The executions of St. Alban, Thomas A Becket, Sir Thomas More,

William Laud and Archbishop Thomas Cranmer are painful reminders that there have been casualties along the way, among those who have sought to meet at fence line boundaries. But for the most part Anglican Christians are famous for making compromises and settlements. Our crowning moment, in the 16th century, when ecclesiastical tensions between English Catholics and English Protestants peaked, was ultimately resolved in what became known as the Elizabethan Settlement. As a result, the Protestant Reformation in Europe produced a Church in England that sounded Protestant but acted Catholic. To this day many visitors in an Episcopal Church (the American continuation of the Church of England) pose the question: are you Catholic or are you Protestant? Perhaps to a fault, we have striven to be a church for all seasons. One of our great divines, Richard Hooker from the sixteenth century, coined the phrase, *via media*, the middle way, as an apt description of who we are. From my vantage point *via media* is Elizabethan jargon for riding the fences.

Today the Episcopal Church is once again embroiled in *via media* pursuits. Socially liberal bishops and staunchly orthodox bishops are obsequiously polite to one another in public despite deep seeded animosities as they seek to mend and maintain unity along common fences. Deep in our ecclesiastical DNA, we affirm the notion that we should be out there riding those fences; maintaining unity; and giving everyone a fair hearing.

I am comfortable with my Anglican heritage. I ride fences all the time, and have done so my whole life. My wife calls me Mr. Gray: another term to describe someone who doesn't like black or white and wants to see truth on both sides. In addition to riding fences, I have driven taxi cabs, failed as an amateur boxer, been a butcher, graduated with a degree in Animal Science from Cal Poly, met the Queen of England, as well as her son Prince Charles, and served as a missionary in the Muslim world for nearly 17 years. My wife is, as it was, from the other side of fence, or as the British say, the other side of the pond. She is from Sweden. None of our four children were born in the United States. My first two boys, ages 16 and 14, were born in Tunisia. My daughter, age 10, was born in Sweden. My youngest son, age five, was born in Casablanca, Morocco.

As a priest, my instincts and job description include fence riding. I am to be out there meeting people in all walks of life and circumstances. There has hardly been a week of my life when I feel that I have failed to meet this challenge. I live in a pluralistic world, full of varying points of view. My job description also includes being selective and exclusive. This is what a priest does when he cultivates and waters his flock. More often than not, the cultivating and watering takes place out there in the center of the pasture land, far from the fence lines. Although my calling is to be out in the world, along the multi-faceted boundaries of our American society, I also have the charge to venture as deeply as I can into the Kingdom of God. It is there that I am to find sustenance for my own soul as well as fodder to nurture those in my care. In my vows as a priest, I promised both "share in the renewing of the world," as well as to "nourish" the Church. As priest I am to be both out there along the fence lines, as well as in the inner recesses of Christian spirituality and the church. It is there, in the center of the pasture, where I have found that the grass is the greenest and most nutritious. Watering holes sometimes are along the fence lines but more often than not they are hours away by horse back.

I haven't always been a priest, however. For me, priesthood didn't happen until age fifty. Up till then I'd been riding a lot of fences. I was born in Glendale, California in 1948. My generation was the first generation to be raised by the television. In fact my family was the first on the block to have a TV. Via the marvel of TV, I was an eye witness to the Dodgers winning the World Series in 1959 and President Kennedy's assassination on my 15th birthday. The television exposed me to frontiers and horizons that my parents did not know about as they grew up. The "I Love Lucy Show", "Truth or Consequences", "Batman" and "The Steve Allen Show" all went into forming my persona and worldview. I learned about religion through the lens of 1960 Hollywood: another frontier I rode alongside.

My father and grandfather owned a wholesale toy business, so I was well ensconced in middle class, capitalist America. I was instructed to embrace Herbert Hoover and rugged individualism as true models of virtue. I always felt that we had the means to live in upper-middle class Los Angeles but my parents unostentatious values determined that we should live in middle class America: Eagle Rock, California to be exact. For my sister and I, Eagle Rock, California was the center of the universe -- all surrounding territories were unfamiliar fence line boundaries.

My mother was a seeker and my father was accommodating. His muted resignation was a model to me of tolerance as my mother engaged herself in a fervent search for truth. Her quest for metaphysical reality intensified each year of her adult life. Her religious pursuit of spiritual veracity brought her along some rather unorthodox fence lines. As a confirmed Episcopalian, she had always maintained loyalty to the church in name. She insisted that my sister and I attend Episcopal Church School during the formative years of our lives. In reality she rarely attended an Episcopal service. Nonetheless, upon this Anglican foundation she built an intricate system of eastern mysticism and traditional Christianity. Her loyalty to the ancient liturgies of the church and her interest in Asian religions created a unique mélange of Buddhist, Hindu and Christian conviction. Today she calls herself a Rosecrucian, but has spent much of her adult life in the Unity Church.

My mother' s New Age gurus of the 1960 s provided fence lines that I was compelled to ride along. I was her son and one does what their mother chooses. My Sundays as a junior higher included some rather unconventional religious services and communities of faith. As a teenager, I didn't buy into the doctrines of reincarnation, vegetarianism, and karma that my mother so zealously embraced. Frankly I thought that it all sounded rather speculative. Despite my independence, my mother did instill in me one value: God answers prayer. Every morning, before I would go off to school my mother and I would pray. Usually the recommended topic of prayer was getting better grades and having the mind of Christ. Getting better grades was a distressing notion for me as a teenager. Having the mind of Christ was pretty esoteric stuff for a sixteen year old. As I look back at those interludes of prayer I suppose that having the mind of Christ meant that my grades could somehow be levitated from a solid 2.5 to a 3.0 by meditation. Despite my best efforts to levitate myself and my grades, I proceeded to bring home solid C+ work; there were some A's, and once in a while a "D" or two. Other than that I had a rather typically American, suburban adolescence.

My father and I played golf and went to track meets: a pleasurable experience for both of us. During the underlying crisis of grades, which persisted throughout my adolescence, I began to suspect that grades were more a matter of study habits than prayer. It didn't seem to me that God and grades were on the same page. Seeds of cynicism towards religion were beginning to grow.

I squeaked into college. I don't think that my 2.6 GPA and my low SAT scores actually qualified me for the California State College system. In fact I was denied entrance at Humbolt State College. California State Polytechnic College gave me the nod. I have often wondered if my entrance was based on a bureaucratic glitch. Perhaps there was a dimpled or pregnant chad on those IBM cards that students were required to fill out. In any event by the end of my first quarter in College, I stunned my parents with a resounding 1.6 GPA. A letter from the college President indicated that unless I brought my GPA up to a 2.0 by the end of the year, I would have to yield my seat at the college to someone else. The thought of being expelled from college created in me visions of laboring as a garbage man or some other menial task for the rest of my life. Within me roared a mighty "no". I can do better than that, I thought. I can remember slamming my fist into my bedroom wall and yelling out at the top of my lungs: I am not going to be a plumber. I hope I don't offend any garbage men or plumbers with this recollection of my college years. I have subsequently discovered that a plumber's knowledge of hydraulic engineering and a sanitation engineer's acquaintance with the intricacies of 21st century recycling far surpass my own.

In college I discovered that I had a pretty good memory and as an animal science major I could memorize my way to academic honors. I made it on the Dean's List and subsequently on the President's List. Accompanying this surge in self initiative, my cynicism about religion became fully matured and I said "hokum" to the church and to Christian faith. It seemed to me that life had more to do with determination and choice than God. I loved, however, exploring the issues of life philosophically, and took every course that the philosophy department offered at Cal Poly, Pomona. I am quite sure that I was the only animal science major that took all my electives in philosophy department. In any event, my new found academic confidence was accompanied by an adamant persuasion of agnosticism. My credo and attitude were simple: who knows if there is a God and in the end who cares. Life goes on fine without God. I declared this my parents. I declared this to my friends. And the more that I declared my agnosticism, the better it felt.

However, along those academic and agnostic fence lines I discovered that I had become a rather lonely person. My search for academic achievements was not paralleled with successes along romantic and social fence lines. In fact I felt as though I was an abject failure in those areas. I fell into a morass of depression. Despite the academic confidence that I had gained, I was plagued with what is popularly known as a "low self image". My life was really rather sheltered. Often I wonder how I might have experimented in a culture more accepting of alternate life-styles. Cal Poly was not a very experimental campus in the 1960 s. In reality I kept my slate pretty clean.

In those days Prozac was not a fence line option for those suffering from depression. My aversion to drugs would probably not have been attractive to me even if medication for depression had been recommended to me by a doctor. My own gut reaction is that medicine would have made little difference for me in the end. However, I did seek a counselor, at our school that proved to be very helpful. Among the topics that I discussed with my therapist was God... He suggested that I consider prayer. Perhaps my ignoring God was part of the reason that I was experiencing such loneliness and isolation.

I began to read the Bible. The Scriptures were a frontier and fence line that I knew very little about. Although I had some exposure to the Bible from Sunday school days, I probably couldn't name ten books in the Bible -- even less about their contents. There were many stories in the Bible that seemed fanciful and extraordinary. Nonetheless, there was something about the narratives of Adam and Eve, Abraham, Isaac and Jacob that connected me with a primal reality. I was compelled to keep reading. Much of the Old Testament seemed extraneous and irrelevant. I couldn't imagine a god who issued condemnations to menstruating women who entered the Temple or anathemas to weavers who mixed flax and wool in the same fabric. I skipped over a lot of the pages of the Old Testament but continued to discover enough sustenance to keep me plodding on. I enjoyed seeing, in the pages of the Bible, men honestly trying to find who they were intended to be and a God who genuinely was interested in their pursuit. It seemed such a crowning honor that God would seek out humankind individually making sure that he not violate their choice or decision. Jacob wrestling with the Angel of God became so contemporary for me. I was still a rather depressive guy but found a lift in my reading of the Bible. By the time I got to the New Testament, I was keen to mull over the notion of as a Good Shepherd, Great Physician or even as a Savior. These metaphors still resonate within me.

Concurrent with my personal investigation of the Bible was a recurring contact with various Christian groups on campus. My first impression of them was that they were brain-washed and overly zealous. I was, however, willing to engage them in conversation. Perhaps my willingness to discuss was an admission in me that recognized some truth in their claims. They were to me, however an odious lot, keen to castigate a great portion of the population to hell (something that I wasn't so eager to do), they also readily believed in things that were hard for a 20th Century college student to accept. Talking donkeys, walking on water, multiplying fish and loaves was certainly beyond the pail of my experience.

Despite such objections I was willing to make some concessions. The first concession that I was willing to make was that perhaps some of my psychological misery was due to the fact that I had been neglecting God. Secondly, I was willing to entertain the thought that in my neglect of God I had lost sight of who he had intended for me to be. Was it possible that Jesus actually overcame the grave and was a present help in my own malaise. I had never read about Pascal's Wager but understood the concept. You can't know unless you try: the leap of faith produces assurance and faith. I took the plunge and prayed a prayer that is written at the back of one of those tracts that campus Christians distribute. I prefaced my prayer with a disclaimer: "God I don' t know if you exist, but if you do I need you. Come into my life, forgive me for neglecting you and be my savior." Amen. I like the word savior because it implies that we don t just need good counsel or advice. Calling someone your savior is an acknowledgment that we need to be rescued.

In that moment I felt as though an inner transaction was made. Mysteriously I found myself alongside fence lines that I had grown up with and somehow once again felt in harmony with. It was like coming home. It felt like I was being held rather than trying to hold my life together all by myself. I also was to discover that I was no longer along the edge of a fence line or at the edge of a boundary. I had ventured out into the center of a pasture land. By deliberate choice I had defined my course and my spirituality location. I had turned in a direction that would radically change my life forever.

The first few years as an adult Christian could best be characterized as zealous devotion. I read, prayed, memorized and attended everything and anything that was suggested that I should read, memorize, attend to or pray about. In the process I came to a fork in the road. Because of prior decisions, I was already enrolled and studying at Southwestern School of Law. It was an enjoyable and challenging endeavor. But there, one day, in the midst of the law library, I was overcome with a tremendous sense of calling. A voice within me was suggesting that I should quit law school and go into the ministry. Within a month I ended my legal studies and was registered to begin at Fuller Theological Seminary in Pasadena, California.

My studies at seminary were some of the happiest days of my life. I loved the environment of study and seeking God. Never before had I met such devotion for excellence and intellectual honesty. It was a treat for me to listen to men and women who had discovered so many things along the fence lines as well as out in the center of the pasture of the church. I look forward to a sabbatical month later this year to return to that life of study.

When seminary was completed I vacillated between going overseas into mission work or remaining in the States. I chose the latter, then the former, then the latter and then the former again. During the ten years following my graduation from seminary, I served as a youth pastor/minister/missionary on three continents. I drove a meat truck as well as a taxi cab, worked as a furniture mover, taught in a Roman Catholic junior high school, directed the Residence Hall of the YMCA in Glendale, CA, served as a youth pastor as well as taught English as a second language in Algiers, worked in the Swedish Lutheran Church and eventually married a Swede in Jonkoping, Sweden. Today we live and are happily married in Turlock, California. I am the Rector of St. Francis Episcopal Church.

Most of the past 25 years, however, have been spent in the Muslim world. I first met Muslims when I ventured out with Young Life, an international Christian youth organization, to France in 1977. There in France I discovered the wonderfully colorful life of the Arabic people living as immigrants in France. At least a third the Young Life Club in Lyon, France was Algerians. Contrary to everything that I had heard or expected, some of these Algerian young men and occasional young women were zealous Christians. They were to me models of joy and enthusiasm, open and motivated to return to their homeland as Christian witnesses.

The challenge of Christian ministry and their zeal intrigued me. I wanted to follow them in that venture and also be a Christian witness in the Muslim world. An intricate series of contacts and friendships that I had developed while in California and France eventually led me to the Anglican Church in Algiers, The Church of the Holy Trinity. There I would live and work for three years, earning money as an English teacher and serving as an assistant to the chaplain. Although I had been ordained in the Congregational Church some five years before, I was accepted as a co-worker in the Anglican Church. I was privileged to meet many ordinary as well as sophisticated individuals. Working and living on the British compound of the Anglican Church and the British Council led me into daily encounters with parking lot attendants as well as high ranking diplomats and Algerian politicians. I even met Queen Elizabeth when she visited Algeria in 1981. It was there that I also met my wife who came from Sweden to Algiers on a path for adventure and new experiences similar to my own.

Two things occurred during those years in Algeria: first, I had to process my own Christian faith through the eyes of people who held a much different world view from my own; secondly, I rediscovered the Anglican traditions that I had grown up with. Holy Trinity Church would become for me a second Christian homecoming: a return to my liturgical and sacramental roots.

In the end, my wife and I have lived and have been in contact with Muslims ever since those days in Algeria. After our three years in Algeria, we spent six years in Tunisia. We then enjoyed a two year break in Sweden because of the Gulf War, but again working and living with Muslims; and subsequently four years in Morocco with The United Bible Societies. Today my sympathies and respect run deeply for the Muslim people. They were the ones who welcomed three of our four children into the world. They were the ones that provided a formative environment for all of our children. The value that they place on hospitality and family loyalties is something that we can learn from in the West. The post 9/11 images of Islam that are fed by images of warfare and strife are not the images that I have safeguarded from my life in the Arab world. Islam is an evangelistic religion, just as Christianity is an evangelistic religion. It is not content to allow religious differences to go by without comment. It is my testimony that I experienced very little tension because of these theological differences. There is a tremendous willingness among Muslims to agree to disagree; at least among those with whom I shared a fence line for 17 years. It is my opinion that the political conflicts that we are so aware of today are much more the result of poverty, injustice and oppression than religion. Religion may provide a convenient medium for frustrations and foment but they are not the cause of conflict. Imagine how Americans would live in a comparable environment. Unemployment in North Africa approaches 50%. In Palestine the figure is 70%. In my mind's eye suicide bombing and guerilla warfare are engendered by a state of desperation and anger towards political realities that seem to insure a state of oppression.

Despite my years in the Muslim world and my respect for the piety of many Muslin friends I was never felt moved to leave my Christian faith. Certainly there are truths in Islam and values that we as Christians would do well to incorporate into our life and practice. For me the liturgy and forms of the church that had long been absent from my life; my years at Fuller Theological Seminary; and especially that prayer years ago in my college dormitory, "Lord be to me a savior," confirmed in me that as I continue to ride along the fences I still am convinced that we need a Savior.

17
KOREAN WAR

Half a league, half a league,
Half a league onward,
All in the valley of Death
Rode the six hundred.
' Forward, the Light Brigade!
Charge for the guns!' He said:
Into the valley of Death
Rode the six hundred.

War was not an uplifting religious experience: it is where I killed people, starting on my first day in combat.

I was on a destroyer in the enemy port of Wonson, blowing it to oblivion, and it was not even a genuine war I was fighting in - this was a United Nations "police action". I was topside on the bridge of the USS Boyd, wearing helmet, life jacket, and a 45 strapped to my side - standard gear for a naval officer aboard a destroyer in enemy waters. Wonson was the North Korean port we had laid siege to now for several weeks. Our ships sailed in with guns blazing, and we established a presence with fire power that the North Koreans could not repulse. Our ships circled with a continual barrage from our five inch guns; we could not be driven out. This was the rail center for North Korea, where the mountains forced everything down to the sea coast. Our siege had created havoc in their supply lines.

In the darkness of night, the enemy moved out in small boats to launch floating mines, which several of our ships hit and sank. We lived in fear of these mines; they opened gapping holes in the hull that could sink a ship so fast that few men made it topside to escape.

Only a month, before I was an NROTC student at the University of Colorado, living in a fraternity house. Then graduation, a commission as naval officer, and orders to this ship in Korean waters. I was hurried across the Pacific, ferried by an ammo ship to Delta Point outside the entrance to Wonson, and passed by rope in a bosom's chair to this destroyer. The Captain was glad to see me: they were operating short of officers, and I had been trained in gun control. He assigned me to Gun Control One, the turret occupying the highest point on the ship from which the gun batteries were visually controlled. My first day aboard ship I was directing fire at enemy targets ashore: so much for orientation and indoctrination.

> **Cannon to right of them,**
> **Cannon to left of them,**
> **Cannon in front of them**
> **Volley'd and thunder'd;**
> **Storm'd at with shot and shell,**
> **Boldly they rode and well,**
> **Into the jaws of Death**
>
> **Into the mouth of Hell,**
> **Rode the six hundred:**

Until this evening, I had felt little fear. From boyhood days when I rode a stick horse with No-Water fighting Indians (or was No-Water fighting the cavalry?), I had always enjoyed the thrill of battle. I watched with envy as two older brothers went off to join the navy in World War Two, but I was too young. Now my chance had come, but the glamour faded fast. The first week we pulled survivors out of the water from a ship that hit a mine and sank. The ship went down so fast that few made it topside, so over 200 men had the horrible death of slow suffocation in the darkness of their coffin beneath the water. We were able to rescue a dozen men we pulled from the water. They stunk from hours in the sea clinging to debris.

Later our destroyer was close to shore shelling rail yards in a port further north, Chogin, when our radio picked up a distress call from a pilot overhead whose plane had been hit by an enemy MIG and he was about to eject. I was on the bridge. We searched the sky for sight of his parachute, and then saw it coming down close to shore. The captain ordered flank speed, and we headed to where the pilot fell into the water, only a couple hundred yards offshore. Just at that moment, the MIG swooped down with his missile exploding on our port side, a near miss. Then a shore battery opened up. As our ship came alongside the downed pilot, the backwash from our propeller caught the parachute he was wearing and dragged him beneath the water. Men dived from the bridge in a rescue effort. The captain ordered me to launch the whaleboat, and I headed to where the men were holding the pilot afloat. Enemy shells were exploding on all sides. I pulled the unconscious pilot into the lifeboat and immediately began mouth-to-mouth resuscitation as the boat returned to the ship. We laid him on the deck and continued efforts at resuscitation. It was of no use: I could see he was dead. Perhaps twenty, his blonde hair and handsome features contrasted with the lifeless aviator's uniform he would wear no more. He was likely some fraternity guy who had come to war like myself. Somewhere there would be a father and mother who would grieve, and maybe a young bride waiting for his next visit home. I looked in his lifeless eyes and realized it was the first dead person I had ever seen close up. I was to see many more.

> " Forward, the Light Brigade! ".
> Was there a man dismay'd?
> Not though the soldier knew
> Some one had blunder'd:
>
> Their's not to make reply,
> Their's not to reason why,
> Their's but to do and die:

Into the valley of Death
Rode the six hundred.

Then back again to Wonson. Our radar suddenly located a small boat -
probably laying mines - and we opened fire. It went down with our first
salvo, but how many mines had it laid first? I looked into the darkness and
wondered. Would we hit a mine as I slept below deck and plummet to our
coffin on the bottom of Wonson Bay? I saw again the face of that dead
aviator, and I knew the emotion of fear. One such day and night lead to
another, on and on, and we were six weeks at sea before returning to a
Japanese port for a couple days of rest, then back again.

Now I was seasoned and expected to undertake one of the assignments
of a junior office - leading a shore party. Our forces had occupied YoDo, a
small island inside Wonson Bay with a hill in its center. A searchlight atop
this hill provided our night planes with an azimuth to help them find targets
and directions for a return to their Carrier offshore. Our ship's mission was
to send a party consisting of an officer, six riflemen, and two radio opera-
tors ashore to climb the hill and man the searchlight, setting the correct
azimuth that was changed every night by secret code. As a junior officer
and expendable, I was sent to YoDo Island many times. Since the searchlight was within range of the enemy guns and an easy target, it often received incoming salvos. I became familiar with the slit trenches on the
hill.

I became acquainted with the English Commandos who occupied the
island. There was also a mysterious civilian who I assumed was CIA. He
went by the name of "Bom Bom English Junior". He joked and made light
of the entire scene, living in a little hut. As he operated the radio, wearing
headphones and talking to a microphone mounted on a tree, he cranked on
a bicycle wheel-like contraption to generate power. It was a weird setup to
go with a weird guy. On some of my visits he was not there, and I learned
that he used a small boat to go to the enemy mainland under cover of darkness and collect the intelligence messages from agents ashore. Some months
later I learned that Bom Bom English Junior had been captured one night

ashore, and was carried through Wonson shackled in a small bamboo cage. I've often wondered what his final days and hours were like.

When can their glory fade?
Oh, the wild charge they made!
All the world wonder'd.
Honor the charge they made!
Honor the Light Brigade,
Noble six hundred!

I had three seven-month tours of duty off the Korean coast. After the first tour I returned for a visit home. My parents had great concern for me as did a few others in town who had someone in Korea, but they were the exceptions. It seemed as if no one else had heard of the war, and few knew where I had been or seemed to care. It was not a war, only a United Nations police action, and few were in full accord with Truman's decision to commit American boys to battle. The nation was still tired from World War Two. I returned to Korea for my second tour; life became drudgery.

My three years of obligatory service came to an end shortly after the Korean Armistice, and I opted to trade my commission for the life of a civilian. As a boy I had considered a naval career, but the long months at sea were too much as I contemplated a lifetime ahead.

Where are the fence lines that define war? As a youngster I had a lot of bravo about fighting, and I longed to be a professional military man. Then I was in a war; it was not an uplifting experience. I aimed guns at humans ashore and pulled the trigger. How many did I kill? Did I kill any women and children? I don't know the answer, and it wasn't a particular concern at the time, because they were all enemy. Then the shells came back in my direction, exploding nearby, meant for me. I saw death close-up, looking into the lifeless eyes of young men killed in action. Had their plans for life included this?

Was my religious faith made stronger by war? I don't know. Aboard the destroyer we had no minister or cleric, it was an amoral existence, and seldom was our godliness improved ashore. On Christmas Eve after six weeks at sea we pulled into the port of Yokusuka, Japan and tied up alongside a cruiser. I went ashore on liberty. Leaving the main gate of the naval base, I walked across the street into the Black Market Alley, a section full of every vice known to man. A banner over the first cabaret proclaimed:

SPECIAL XMAS STRIP SHOW.

My religious faith had not yet sunk that low. I returned to the ship, went aboard the cruiser alongside, and celebrated midnight Mass at an altar setup under the gun turrets. I knelt on the steel deck, and again found a genuine moment of prayer. That fence line was getting mended.

18

THE URBAN COWBOY

My early job riding fences on the ranch was good training for a career as a business executive riding jets around the world. I was still in the saddle doing the same sort of things, and only the names and culture had changed.

I completed college and began work for Owens-Illinois, a company who produced glass containers and other packaging. The products held little glamour, but they were the ultimate in mass production; the company and its affiliates produced one-half the bottles in the world. My baptism came in a factory that produced three million bottles a day, operating around the clock with machines that never stopped. The factory had two thousand workers and one thousand were females, mostly working mothers. There was constant turmoil over work assignments, termination, overtime, and automation. The union president would often be waiting when I arrived at 6 am to argue some controversy.

The normal day-to-day job as a manager was a constant challenge, but nothing had prepared me for the vortex that arose as the nation became engulfed during the 60's "Decade of Dissent" with the Vietnam War, underground subversive activities, racial discrimination, race riots, union strikes, and equal pay for women. I had all these issues on my plate nearly every day. Vietnam anti-war protesters held their march against the Oakland Army Base, and riots made it difficult to get to the factory for work. The National Guard was called out; we drove through manned barricades. The protests were carried into the factory by militant radicals who taunted management. Smoke filled the air from race riots as young Blacks touched businesses down the street. A Black Caucus of militant employees stomped into my office demanding that I correct the injustice of racial discrimination. Women's equal pay and job rights were beginning to fester, and rightly so. When I started in the plant there was not a single woman among the thousand who had advanced above the entry level job, and I promoted the first one in the company to the salaried foreman level. Undercover police found our machine department was awash in a sea of drugs, mostly heron. Foremen fired workers who were openly smoking marijuana on the job. Yes, it was a swirling vortex.

After twenty years of factory experience, I moved to the corporate headquarters, where I became the Manager of Quality Assurance with thirty glass factories and sales offices located from coast to coast. We dominated the market place, but had one major failing - quality problems - my new area of responsibility. I inherited a weak organization and was instructed to hire a strong staff then mandate those things that needed changed, and to let heads roll when required. Quality became a battle ground for several years; I was the man out on point. Factory managers fought to defend their sacred territory, but I had a mandate from top management. So I challenged plants that had unacceptable quality, and I won every battle. In the first two years we removed six plant managers from their jobs, which sent an unmistakable message. Soon I was able to speak softly because everyone knew I carried a big stick; we gradually moved from hard sell, stuffing it down the throat, to soft sell, building on teamwork and participatory management. Within three years our company had become the undisputed world-wide quality leader.

Then I became involved with the international operations which had factories in 32 foreign countries. In the course of ten years I traveled to 50 factories in twenty countries to provide on-site assistance.

During my management career two social issues dominated the workplace: how to successfully integrate Blacks into a racist climate, and the glass ceiling for females. Other ethical issues involved safety, aggressive strategies against small competitors, and ruthless personnel policies to improve the profit margins? Often times the answers were not clear. The manager had to reach back to find something in his saddlebag for help; it was like riding the fence line on the 7-11 ranch when I had to spur the horse up the rocky trail to get to a broken fence, improvise with the tools I carried in my saddle bag, fix it, and get back off the mountain before dark in time to do the evening chores. Some priorities never change.

19
A COWBOY'S PRAYER

My first job was working as a cowboy on the 7-11 ranch west of Buffalo Gap. Unlike the glamour portrayed by Hollywood, it was a tough and lonely life; a hard day's work was followed by the loneliness of a night watching campfire embers die. Badger Clark, poet laureate of South Dakota, was also a cowboy during his early years. Here are some lines from a poem he wrote about that life.

> Oh Lord, I've never lived where churches grow.
> I love creation better as it stood
> That day You finished it so long ago
> And looked upon Your work and called it good.
>
> I know that others find You in the light
> That's sifted down through tinted window panes,
> And yet I seem to feel You near tonight
> In this dim quiet starlight on the plains
> ....
> Forgive me, Lord, if sometimes I forget.
> You know about the reasons that are hid.
> You understand the things that gall and fret;
> You know better than my mother did.
> Just keep an eye on all that's done and said
> And right me, sometimes, when I turn aside,
> And guide me on the long, dim trail ahead
> That stretches upward toward the Great Divide.

20
DENOUEMENT
WHAT IF?

Most of us inherit our religion and our cultural traditions. I was raised in frontier towns of western Dakota by parents whose mixed Catholic/ Methodist marriage was hewn to the harsh realities of an impoverished existence and small town life. That gave me much of the religious/cultural baggage I have carried through life. But what if?

What if I'd been born into the Muslim family my youngest daughter lived with as an exchange student in Indonesia? I would have spent my life living the Islamic religious faith, knelt five times each day in prayer to Allah, and made my pilgrimage to Mecca. Twenty percent of the world's populations are Muslim; few worshipers have more zeal; they believe passionately in their God, Allah; profess their faith five times every day as they kneel in the direction of Mecca to pray. If I'd been born in the Muslim culture, would I have been seen as different in the eyes of God? Which God: the Muslim Allah, or my Christian Yahweh?

What if I were born of Jewish parents like my college roommate? I would have attended the synagogue, prayed to Jehovah, worn my skull cap, and follow what was written in the Talmud. If I'd been born a Jew instead of Christian, would I have been a different person as seen in the eyes of God, and which God: Jehovah or Yahweh?

Or what if I was born a Buddhist in the family my oldest daughter lived with in Thailand, or in the Yamoaka family in a Japanese internment camp in California? I would have been a Buddhist. I would enter my temple to quietly meditate, finger my beads, chant my mantra, and try to reach that spiritual plateau of the Nirvana. From my Catholic traditions that would have been an easy stretch for me, because so much of the Buddhist religious experience is the same as my own.

If I had been born a Sioux Indian, living with No-Water in the shadow of the Black Hills, I would have wondered at the spirits of lightening and thunder from those mountain peaks; I would have danced the Ghost dances; climbed to the crest of Bear Butte to kneel in wonderment at my vision of the White Buffalo - a God who could restore my destiny of a tribal life on the plains of Dakota.

What if I'd been raised by an agnostic mother on the wharves of San Francisco, and believed all that religious stuff was superstition and bunk? If there is a God and a Heaven, would I forfeit my opportunity because I had no religious faith?

Having been raised as a part-time Protestant in my youth, I feel entirely comfortable when I attend their Evangelical services. Is the Protestant God I pray to in their Born Again service the same one I pray to in my Catholic church?

I have often wondered, does the same God serve all these religious faiths and also the infidels with no faith? Is our Christian God, Yahweh, the same guy as Jehovah of the Jews, and Allah of the Muslims? If not, then he must be a strange God to exclude so many. Which of us are left stranded and hopeless on the parapet? If all the same God, then he must be sad to see his people so fragmented and squabbling over dogma, fighting about a protocol for worship.

AD COELUM

At the Muezzin's call for prayer,
The kneeling faithful thronged the square,
And on Pushkara's lofty height
The dark priest chanted Brahmna's might.
Amid a monastery's weeds
An old Franciscan told his beads,
While to the synagogue there came
A Jew, to praise Jehovah's name.
The one great God looked down and smiled
And counted each his loving child;

For Turk and Brahmin, monk and Jew
Had reached him through the Gods they knew.

Tradition! Where is the connection between a religious faith and tradition? For any one of us, how much of the religion we profess comes from the culture and the traditions with which we were raised, and how much of it comes from a genuine understanding of our spiritual being? This nebulous tie is addressed in the Broadway musical, Fiddler On the Roof, which takes place in the southern Russia of 1905, the setting of much ethnic and religious strife. The old patriarch of the Jewish clan, Tevye, ponders how his people keep their balance through such turbulent times. His response: tradition!

"We have traditions for everything - how to eat, how to sleep, how to wear clothes. For instance, we always keep our heads covered and always wear a little prayer shawl. This shows our constant devotion to God. You may ask, how did this tradition start? I'll tell you - I don't know! But it's a tradition. Because of our traditions, everyone knows who he is and what God expects him to do."

Whether pauper or king, we each must ultimately reach beyond the confines of our inherited culture to resolve the riddle of life's meaning; make this hardest of all journeys, the search for a God, by ourselves; and find it within our own frail being. After I left the Dakota culture I inherited and traveled through the outside world, I encountered the mores and dogmas of other cultures and religious traditions that have evolved into armed camps through centuries of conflict. Riding those fence lines has been a tough day's work.

BIBLIOGRAPHY

Abbott, E.C. *We Pointed Them North*, University of Oklahoma Press, 1939, pg. 28

Armstrong, Karen. *A History of God*, Ballentine Books, NY 1993, Pg. 276, 277, 281, 317

Brown, Dee. *Bury My Heart At Wounded Knee*, Holt, Rinehart 1971, poem in Public Domain

"Buddha*,*" *Modesto Bee*, April 14, 1996

Buddhism*, The Random House Dictionary of the English Language*, Random House, 1970

Buffalo Gap Centennial 1886 - 1986, Centennial committee, 1986

Bye, John O. *Back Trailing*, Alexander Printing Company, 1956, pg. 38

Catron, Marge. *Camp Crook Centennial*, Range Gazette, Pg. 75

Clark, Badger. *Sun and Saddle Leather*, poem now in the public domain

Colliers Encyclopedia, "Abraham", 1960, Vol. 1, pg. 24

Colliers Encyclopedia, "Arabic Literature", 1960, Vol. 2, Pg. 31

Colliers Encyclopedia, "Buddhism", 1960, Vol. 4, pg. 21

Colliers Encyclopedia, "Byzantine, Pg. 153

Colliers Encyclopedia, "Christianity", Pg. 60

Colliers Encyclopedia, "Eastern Orthodox Church", Vol. 6, Pg. 473

Colliers Encyclopedia, "Iran", Vol 10 p. 405

Colliers Encyclopedia, "Islam", 1960, Vol. 10, Pg. 465

Colliers Encyclopedia, "Jesus", Vol. 10, Pg. 678, 680, 681

Colliers Encyclopedia, "Paul", 1960, Vol. 15. Pg. 114

Colliers Encyclopedia, "Peter", 1960, Vol. 11, Pg. 738

Colliers encyclopedia, "Reformation". 1960, Pg. 304

Colliers Encyclopedia, "Venice", Vol. 19, Pg. 133

Custer County History, Custer County Historical Society, 1977

Dimont, Max. *Jews, God and History*, Signet Books, 1962, Pg. 15, 29, 27, 118, 172, 181, 225, 226, 227

Dugan, Bill. *Crazy Horse*, Harpers Paperbacks, 1992

Encarta 97 Encyclopedia, "Shinto", Microsoft, 1997

Encarta Encyclopedia, "Islam", Microsoft, 1997

Encarta Encyclopedia, "Literature of Buddhism", Microsoft, 1997

"Evangelical", *Random House Dictionary of the English Language*, Random House, Inc., NY 1970

"Evangelicalism", Encarta 97, Microsoft 1997

Grotier Encyclopedia Inc., "Islam", 1997

Holy Bible, St. Matthew, Ch. 6

"Islam*"*, *The Random House Dictionary of the English Language*, Random House 1980

Johnstone and Mandryk*, Operation World*, Paternoster Lifestyle, UK 2001, Pg 2

Josephus, Flavius. *Antiquities of the Jews*, (As translated from the original Greek by William Whiston, Professor of Mathematics, University of Cambridge), J.B. Alden Publisher, 1890, Book XV11, Chap. V, AD 36, Pg. 79.

Judaism, *The Random House Dictionary of the English Language*, Random House 1970

L'Amour, Louis. *The Walking Drum*, Bantam Books, 1984, p. 171

Litt. D. From Ryukoku University in Jodo Studies.

Modesto Bee, Dennis Robins, Staff writer, 4/14/96

Modesto Bee, Mark Pinsky, 11/23/96

Norris, Kathleen. *Dakota*, Houghton Miffin Company, 1993, pg. 1.

Paul II, Pope John. *Crossing the Threshold of Hope*, Alfred A. Knopf, 1994, Pg. 46, 47, 148, 151

"Philosophy", *Modesto Bee*, April 14, 1996

"Protestantism", Encarta 97, Microsoft, 1997

"Religion", *The Random House Dictionary of the English Language*, Random House, 1980

Robison, Gordon. *Arab Gulf States*, Lonely Planet Publications, Australia, 10/96, pg. 26, 28

Romaine, Harry. *The Best Loved Poems of the American People*, Doubleday, 1936, Poem in Public Domain

Stein, Joseph. Lyrics by Sheldon Harnick, *Fiddler on the Roof*, Simon & Schuster, 1965

Telushkin, Rabbi Joseph. *Jewish Literacy*, William Morrow and Company, 1991, pg. 125, 140

Telushkin, Rabbi Joseph. *Jewish Literacy*, William Morrow, 2001. Pg. 3, 11, 27

The Economist, "Mushroom Cloud". Feb. 25, 1995

The Saint Andrew Daily Missal, E.M. Lohmann Co., 1943, Pg. 523

U.S.A. TODAY, "Religion in America, 4/1/96

Wells, H.G. *The Outline of History*, Doubleday, 3rd Rev., 1949, pg. 189, 190, 381, 395, 398, 404, 528, 530, 538, 540, 541, 545, 552, 601, 611, 690, 742